ChatGPT in ESL Education:

From CALL 3.0 toward CALL 4.0 or on the edge of the event horizon of an AI black hole?

Yeungnam University Press
280 Daehak-ro, Gyeongsan-si, Gyeongsangbuk-do 38541, Republic of Korea
Tel. +82-53-810-1802~4
Fax. +82-53-810-4722

https://book.yu.ac.kr

Cover design and illustration by Chae Yeong Lee

First published 17th January 2025
Printed in Republic of Korea at the University Press, Gyeongsan

ISBN 978-89-7581-601-7 93740

ChatGPT in ESL Education:

From CALL 3.0 toward CALL 4.0 or on the edge of the event horizon of an AI black hole?

Kwang Hee Hong

Yeungnam University Press

To

KKang-ee and KiKi

Acknowledgements

I would like to dedicate this book to Keiko K. Samimy (1952-2023), a meticulous ESL researcher with rigor, a guided ESL teacher educator with a warm heart, and a supportive colleague with enthusiasm. Part of this book, specifically concerning AI and CALL, stemmed from our discussions about the prospective roles of ESL teachers within the expanding environment of digital technologies in the early 2009. I am deeply grateful to Dr. Sangjo Lee in the Department of Physics at Yeungnam University in Korea, who provided numerous explanations that helped me interpret mathematical expressions in AI materials and express them in plain language. He also imparted diverse insights as a natural scientist on the current and future developments in AI throughout our year-long discussions. My gratitude extends to two visual artists, Ms. Giyoung Yun and Ms. Chae Yeong Lee, for their diligent work in creating or adapting figures throughout the book. Giyoung created the figure of Turing Test, while Chae Yeong replicated and adapted figures of neurons, neural models, deep learning models, information processing, and data scalability. Chae Yeong also designed the image for the book cover.

Preface

Late in the afternoon on the day when the manuscript of this book was sent to the university press, news alerts kept popping up in my iPhone, headlined 'the 2024 Nobel Prize winners in Physics and Chemistry: John J. Hopfield and Geoffrey E. Hinton for Physics, and David Baker for Chemistry.' All three are leading AI scientists whose work has marked a significant epoch in the history of AI development. The contributions of Hopfield and Hinton are discussed throughout the book, particularly in the chapters covering the history of AI, its features, and its benefits and drawbacks. Indeed, we have transcended the era of 'humans and computers' and are now crossing the border into the new era of 'humans and AI.'

The primary goal of this book is to inform pre-service and in-service ESL educators, as well as ESL researchers, about ChatGPT, or generative AI, including its origins, key features, and its parallels to conceptual understanding in principal SLA (Second Language Acquisition) theories. These will help the ESL educators enhance their understanding of how ChatGPT can generate human language. In addition, it proposes the need for a new conceptual and pedagogical framework of Computer-Assisted Language Learning (CALL) within the ESL domain. Specifically, the latter parts of the book serve as an open forum for the ESL educators to discuss critical perspectives on both the benefits and drawbacks of AI. While this book is primarily intended for professionals in second language education, individuals in other fields will find it accessible and relevant, as it addresses common concerns about integrating generative AI into various disciplines.

In their acceptance speech, Hopfield and Hinton conveyed 'fear and warning' to the public, rather than 'hope,' due to the potential risks associated with AI. As Bertrand Russell once stated, "Uncertainty, in the presence of vivid hopes and fears, is painful but must be endured if we wish to live without the support of comforting fairy tales." We all need to make a collective effort to wisely address the new emerging entity, as our ancestors have done throughout human history.

October 2024
Starbucks at the Main Library, YU
Gyeongsan, Korea

Contents

> The sciences have developed in an order the reverse of what might have been expected. What was most remote from ourselves was first brought under the domain of law, and then, gradually, what was nearer: first the heavens, next the earth, then animal and vegetable life, then the human body, and last of all (as yet very imperfectly) the human mind.
>
> (Russell, 1997/1935, p. 49)

Introduction

The emergence of ChatGPT, or generative AI (Artificial Intelligence), signals a seismic shift in the landscape of education. This new entity, arising from advancements in various fields of academia and digital technology, fascinates not only ESL teachers and learners but also those in other content areas with its unprecedented performance.[1] Such remarkable performance has been well reflected in the phenomenal response from the public worldwide since its disclosure in November 2022 (Duarte, 2024; Mollman, 2022), including its benefits to general education (Heaven, 2023a; Johnson, 2023), medicine (Bajaj, 2024; Faust, 2023; Lee, Goldberg, & Kohane, 2023; Mun & Koh, 2022; Omar et al., 2024), business (Haelein

1 Technically, ChatGPT is a type of generative AI based on a large language model (cf. Aggarwal, 2023, pp. 451-453; Prince, 2023, p. 407, Wolfram, 2023). In this book, the terms, ChatGPT, generative AI, and AI, are used interchangeably. For general explanation of generative AI for non-AI professionals, see McKinsey & Company (2024).

& Kaplan, 2019; Kaplan, 2022; Sana, 2024a), arts (Williams, 2024), and various fields in ESL education (e.g., Fathi & Rahimi, 2024; Lee & Lee, 2024; Shin & Lee, 2023; Wang & Gayed, 2024).

Meanwhile, there is a growing tendency among scientists and educators not to view generative AI merely as a machine under the control of *Homo sapiens*, but to treat it as a potential candidate for a new species with intelligence that may pose a threat to human beings (cf. 60 Minutes, 2023a; Center for AI Safety Team, 2024; Li, 2023; Russell, 2019; University of Oxford, 2024; University of Toronto, 2023). The escalating concern is not solely the responsibility of AI scientists[2]; it should also be addressed by ESL professionals. The performance of ChatGPT is not far from ESL education, as it produces the English language with almost perfect accuracy and fluency, largely overlapping what ESL teachers and learners do (Else, 2023; Fathi & Rahimi, 2024; Frank, 2023; Liang et al., 2023). Additionally, a significant distinction between ChatGPT and previous CALL (Computer-Assisted Language Learning) applications is the level of agency involved (cf. Godwin-Jones, 2024; Warschauer & Xu, 2024). In traditional CALL environments, ESL teachers and learners could exert control or participate actively as agents. However, with ChatGPT,

---

2 "In the public eye, there is sometimes confusion between the terms "artificial intelligence" and "machine learning." Machine learning is a subfield of AI that studies the ability to improve performance based on experience. Some AI systems use machine learning methods to achieve competence, but some do not" (Russell & Norvig, 2021, p. 1, quotation marks in original). For various definitions of AI, see Russell & Norvig (2010, pp. 1-2).

such direct involvement might become less essential in the near future (cf. Bengio, 2023; Bengio, LeCun, & Hinton, 2021; Mitchell, 2024; Patel, 2023; Wolfram, 2023).

In line with this considerable wave of change spurred by ChatGPT, a wide array of ESL studies has been conducted on the practical applications of ChatGPT and other generative AI variants (cf. Fathi & Rahimi, 2024; Lee & Lee, 2024; Warschauer & Xu, 2024; Woo et al., 2024). Notably, an increasing number of ESL educators around the world are motivated to integrate generative AI into their classes in various ways and to establish this practice as part of their classroom instruction and curricula (e.g., KATE, 2023, 2024; KOSETA, 2024; PKETA & GETA, 2024). However, there remains a lack of research on fundamental and conceptual issues associated with the use of generative AI by both ESL teachers and learners. These issues include (1) understanding how the features of ChatGPT function, (2) identifying aspects of ChatGPT that can be conceptually related to ESL teaching and learning, (3) recognizing any risks that ESL professionals should consider when using it and (4) determining any necessary precautions they should take. Addressing the issues helps ESL professionals gain better insights into using ChatGPT, leading to more informed and guided use of ChatGPT in their instruction.

Given this, the present work aims to bridge the gap between empirical ESL studies on the practical applications of ChatGPT and the considerations ESL professionals should take into account from their own perspective. Both conceptual considerations and relevant empirical studies on AI in ESL education could help to shed light on many questions that educators face and provide both practitioners and researchers with a dazzling array of conceptual and empirical insights on AI and ESL education (Frank, 2023; Godwin-Jones, 2024; Pack & Maloney, 2023, 2024; Warschauer & Xu, 2024). In this sense, this book serves to contribute to the fulfillment of ESL professionals' aspiration to further understand generative AI and to use it effectively in their instruction.

To this end, this book consists of two parts: (1) A chronicle of the evolutionary development of AI (Chapter 1), followed by an exploration of ChatGPT's mechanisms and features with respect to ESL instruction (Chapter 2, 3, 4); (2) a historical overview of the development of CALL in the domain of ESL, and an examination of AI's prospective role in the domain of both ESL and CALL (Chapter 5). Specifically, the first part overviews how the recent achievements of AI have been made over the past decades and explores the underlying mechanism of AI – not from technical perspectives but from ESL educational perspectives. This aims to provide ESL professionals with a better understanding of AI. As frequently quoted, "[t]he impartiality of history is not that of the mirror, which merely reflects objects, but of the judge, who sees, listens, and decides."[3] Following the historical overview, the underlying mechanisms and features of ChatGPT are discussed within the context of artificial neural networks, informed by the voice of leading AI researchers as captured in their works. The second part examines how CALL has evolved since computers were first introduced into ESL education, and how to integrate the emerging entity, AI, within the domain of CALL. And it is also

3 The quote by Alphonse de Lamartine (1790-1869).

concerned with AI's role in both CALL and ESL education, focusing on what needs to be considered for ESL teachers in a future CALL environment where AI coexists with ESL teachers and learners.

Part I

CHAPTER 1

The Chronicles of AI: Turing, Perceptron, and Deep learning

No matter how trivial it may be, there is always a group of people who love it, study it, and experiment with it. These people are scattered around the world, living their daily lives, yet they often find themselves wanting to exchange detailed information and small discoveries, or cautiously boast about them. Therefore, long before the development of the internet, this group of people knew of each other's existence through various channels, and promised to meet regularly. They liked living that way. Even as time passed, they continued to enjoy living that way. And, they all have one thing in common: digging a small, deep hole straight down.

(Hukuoka, 2009, p. 6)[4]

4 The book was originally published in Japanese; the Japanese excerpt is translated in

In the beginning of a long journey to discuss the genesis of the universe, Tonelli (2021) sanguinely imagines that Neanderthals living in Europe 40,000 years ago created various symbols (e.g., paints on cave walls) and used them directly or indirectly to tell their stories from generation to generation. He confidently states that the ancient tradition continues to go all the way down to the present. A historical overview of the development of AI since the early 1900s tells us a story: A story with imagination, hope, disgruntlement, rigor, tension, aspiration, collaboration and triumph (cf. "AI Winter," 2024; Bostrom, 2014, pp. 1-62; Crick, 1995, pp. 177-199; Glover, 2023; Li, 2023, pp. 147-178; Russell & Norvig, 2021, pp. 5-30; Zizu, 2018).

In this story, there appears not the ancient symbols but a modern craft, *thinking machine*. Depending on story tellers in the field of philosophy, psychology and computer science, the beginning of the story varies from the ancient Greek philosophers (e.g., Aristotle), the philosophers or mathematicians in the 16th and 17th century (e.g., Hobbes and Descartes) to the modern scientists (cf. Russell & Norvig, 2021, pp. 5-17). Although many scholars are said to philosophically and conceptually contribute to the birth of the thinking machine in the history of science, Turing (1950) is commonly regarded as the starting point of its story from both epistemological and ontological point of view (Larson, 2021, pp. 9-17; Russell & Norvig, 2021, pp. 17-30; The Alan Turning Institute, 2023).

English for this book.

In his seminal study, Turing (1950, p. 433) began with a question, "Can machines think?" In pursuit of an answer, he introduced imaginary scenarios, "*the imitation game,*"[5] reflecting the relationship between "machine" and "think." The study is widely considered to have triggered a systematic examination of a long-lasting inquiry in human history: Whether we can create something capable of thinking like us. At the same time, it provides philosophical and conceptual food for thought on 'what the meaning of a thinking machine is' and 'what kinds of theoretical and empirical frameworks are needed to develop such a machine' (cf. Dennett, 1981/1978, pp. 190-229; Gunderson, 1985/1971; Russell & Norvig, 2010, pp. 1020-1033; Searle, 1980; Simon, 2019/1969).

To humans, *thinking* is so natural that everyone takes it for granted; the ownership of the word 'thinking' belongs exclusively to us. Thus, applying it to non-humans sounds awkward and is hard to interpret: The little iron can think like us. Turing (1950) helped us boldly overcome these audiolingual and semantic awkwardness by proposing a thought experiment[6], widely known as *Turing Test* (pp. 433-435).

Simply put, as presented in Figure 1, the context of the Turing Test involves a conversation among three interlocutors. The woman in Room A is an interviewer, while the computer

5 The title of a popular Hollywood film, *The Imitation Game* (Tyldum, 2014), originates from the section title of the paper (Turing, 1950, p. 433, italic in original). For further philosophical discussion of the imitation game, see Gunderson (1985/1971, pp. 39-59).

6 The term, a thought experiment (or *Gedankenexperiment*), simply refers to "a hypothetical scenario that helps us understand things," including an esoteric theory, inaccessible empirical evidence, or a philosophical conundrum (Brysbaert & Rastle, 2009, p. 222).

Figure 1. Visual presentation of Turing Test: the woman in Room A is an interviewer and interviewees in Rooms B and C. The interviewer has no idea about who is in Rooms B and C.

in Room B and the man in Room C are interviewees. She has no idea who is in Rooms B and C. The woman asks a series of questions on various topics to Rooms B and C via the computer on her desk and receives answers through her computer from both rooms. If the answers from both rooms are perfect and the woman observes no anomalies, then couldn't we say that the computer in Room B can think like the man in Room C? Simple as it is, the test compels us to ponder over a new conceptual perspective to understand the idea of thinking machines (Dennett, 1981/1978, pp. 190-229; Gunderson, 1985/1971; Searle, 1980; Simon, 2019/1969). Moreover, it clearly conveys that the notion of *thinking* is not reserved solely for human beings but can also be applied to a non-living thing, provided it performs perfectly like us.

A group of researchers extended Turing's initiative into the theoretical and practical development of a machine that can think like a human being. Organized by McCarthy, researchers from different disciplines scientifically discussed thinking machines at the Dartmouth Workshop, and gave a birth to the term, Artificial Intelligence ("Dartmouth Workshop," 2024; McCarthy et al, 1955; Zizu, 2018).[7] The ultimate purpose of the workshop is clearly presented in the beginning of their proposal.

> The study is to proceed on the basis of the conjecture that every aspect of learning or any other feature of intelligence can in principle be so precisely described that a machine can be made to simulate it. An attempt will be made to find how to make machines use language, form abstractions and concepts, solve kinds of problems now reserved for humans, and improved themselves. We think that a significant advance can be made in one or more of these problems if a carefully selected group of scientists work on it together for a summer. (McCarthy et al., 1955, p. 1)

Although the achievement and contribution made through the workshop are numerous in the history of AI, two aspects are particularly noteworthy from ESL educator's point of view: (1) the development of AI began through "*consilience*"[8]

---

7 Also see for a short summary of Dartmouth Workshop https://home.dartmouth.edu/about/artificial-intelligence-ai-coined-dartmouth

8 In this book, I prefer the term "*consilience*," originally proposed by Wilson (1999). It is used in the general sense of 'interdisciplinarity,' although, technically, the meanings of the two terms are not identical (Wilson, 1999). The development of AI, from its inception to the present, extends beyond mere cooperation among different disciplines (cf. Crick, 1995, pp. 177-199; Laird, 2019; Li, 2023, pp. 147-206; Russell & Norvig, 2021, pp. 1-30; Zizu, 2018). The broad meaning of "*consilience*" is "the key to unification. I prefer this word over "coherence" because its rarity has preserved its precision, whereas coherence has several

of experts from different disciplines (e.g., mathematics, psychology, physics, biology, economics, computer science, etc.) around the world, as Laird (2019, p. xiv) remarks, "the beauty of how these fit together"; and (2) the foundation was laid for subsequent AI research that continues to the present (cf. Arts & Science – University of Toronto, 2024; Crick, 1995, pp. 177-199; Haenlein & Kaplan, 2019; Laird, 2019; Li, 2023, pp. 147-206; Sana, 2024b; Simon, 2019/1969, pp. 1-24).[9]

Following the Dartmouth Workshop, the U.S. Navy disclosed a computer equipped with an initial version of AI in the late 1950s, called *Perceptron*, which was designed by F. Rosenblatt, an American psychologist (Rosenblatt, 1958).[10] The excitement about this achievement and the expectations for the future were vividly described in the title of a New York

possible meanings, only one of which is consilience. ⋯ consilience, literally a "jumping together" of knowledge by the linking of acts and fact-based theory across disciplines to create a common groundwork of explanation" (Wilson, 1999, p. 8, quotation marks in original).

9 In personal conversations with many non-AI professionals, including educators, businessmen, and workers, it appears that they often perceive AI development as exclusively handled by computer scientists and mathematicians, due to the strong association between AI and computers, which are fundamentally rooted in mathematics. However, the *consilience* seen in the Dartmouth Workshop was not a one-time occurrence; it continues to influence current AI development. Among numerous examples, refer to Li (2023, pp. 147-206) for a recent instance of how AI scientists draw inspiration to overcome obstacles – specifically, visual recognition by machines – through *consilience.*

10 In the early 1940s, before Rosenblatt's Perceptron, the neural system of the human brain was mathematically represented by two American scholars, McCulloch and Pitts (1943). They proposed a mathematical model in which mathematical logic was applied to the behavior of neural networks. In other words, their model suggested that the human brain's electrical activity could be understood through principles of computation, which served as the foundation for conceptual frameworks in AI research development (cf. Piccinini, 2020, pp. 107-127).

Times article at the time: "New Navy Device Learns by Doing: Psychologist Shows Embryo of Computer Designed to Read and Grow Wiser" (UPI, 1958). Four parts of the title catch the eyes of the ESL educator: 'learns by doing,' 'embryo,' 'read,' and 'grow wiser.' While the article delivered the news of a machine with new abilities, the expressions used were more akin to describing an infant prodigy than a non-living thing. This is much clearer in the detailed explanation that follows:

> The embryo ⋯ learned to differentiate between right and left after fifty attempts in the Navy's demonstration for newsmen. The service said it would use this principle to build the first of its Perceptron thinking machines that will be able to read and write. It is expected to be finished in about a year ⋯ In the first fifty trials, the machine made no distinction between them. It then started registering a "Q" for the left squares and "O" for the right squares. ⋯ [Dr. Rosenblatt] said the computer had undergone a "self-induced change in the wiring diagram." The first Perceptron will have about 1,000 electronic "association cells" receiving electrical impulses from an eye-like scanning device with 400 photo-cells. The human brain has 10,000,000,000 responsive cells, including 100,000,000 connections with the eyes. (UPI, 1958, quotation marks in original).[11]

What is captivating is that the learning process of the

11 "The perceptron algorithm was originally implemented using hardware circuits. ⋯ [It was] the Mark I perceptron machine built in 1958" (Aggarwal, 2023, p. 9). For further reading about the Mark I perceptron, see Bishop and Biship (2023, p. 18) and National Museum of American History at https://americanhistory.si.edu/collections/nmah_334414

Perceptron is quite similar to how a child learns something new: The child tries it several times, grasps it, and then performs it correctly (Keil, 2006). The only differences are that one is a machine and the other is a human, and the number of cells (i.e., neurons) between them: one thousand electronic cells for the Perceptron and ten billion biological neurons for the human.

The Perceptron inspired AI researchers to raise the anchor and hoist the sails, catching the warm summer wind and propelling the field toward more advanced thinking machines. However, unexpectedly, "winter was coming."[12] They soon faced a severe winter storm, and many of them became lost (cf. "AI Winter," 2024; Bostrom, 2014, pp. 4-14; Fetch.ai, 2024a; Glover, 2023; Russell, 2019, pp. 3-6)[13].

In 1969, about ten years after the Perceptron, American mathematician and computer scientist M. Minsky published a book co-authored with his colleague, S. A. Papert, titled *Perceptrons*, named after the Perceptron (Knight, 2016; Minsky & Papert, 2017/1969). Explaining both the optimistic mood of that time, driven by the Perceptron, and its technical weaknesses, Crick (1995) illustrated the significant repercussions of the book

---

12 The quoted expression tweaks a popular line, "Winter is coming," in an American TV show, *Game of Thrones* (David, Weiss, & Patten, 2011).

13 Researchers in AI communities use the term, *AI winter*, to describe a period when "general interest in the artificial intelligence industry cools, both in terms of funding and public attention" (Glover, 2023). Interestingly, the Dartmouth workshop was held in summer, and the Perceptron was introduced to the public during a summer as well. In the history of AI since Turing (1950), there have been two AI winters: the first from the early 1970s until the early 1980s, and the second from the late 1980s until the mid-1990s ("AI Winter," 2024; Fetch.ai, 2024a, 2024b, 2024c; Glover, 2023; Russell & Norvig, 2021, pp. 22-24).

on the history of AI.

> … The way it worked was that the Perceptron could respond to the task in only two ways: true or false. All it had to be told was whether its (tentative) answer was correct or not. It then altered its connections according to a certain rule, called the Perceptron Learning Rule. Rosenblatt proved that for a certain class of simple problems, those called "linearly separable," it could learn to behave correctly after a finite number of trials. This result attracted a lot of attention because of its mathematical elegance. Unfortunately, its influence was damped by Marvin Minsky and Seymour Papert, who proved that the Perceptron architecture and learning rule could not execute the "exclusive OR" (i.e., apples OR oranges, but not both) and therefore could not learn it. They wrote a whole book expanding on the Perceptron's limitations. This killed interest in Perceptrons for a number of years (Minsky admitted later that it was overkill) and most theoretical work during that time focused on A.I. approaches. (p. 181, quotation marks in original)[14]

Furthermore, in the early 1970s, a review paper, commonly known as the Lighthill Report in the AI community, was published on the state of AI research at that time (cf. Agar, 2020; Lighthill, 1973, McCarthy, 2000). Although the report provided a review of AI research and proposed guiding directions for future AI development, it criticized what AI research had

14 Also see Bernstein (1981) for Minsky's other works, the path he had traversed as an AI scientist, his relationship with Rosenblatt, and the glacially slow yet steadily advancing milieu within AI communities in the 1970s.

achieved so far, concluding

> 3 Past disappointment: Most workers in AI research in related fields confess to a pronounced feeling of disappointment in what has been achieved in the past twenty-five years. Workers entered the field around 1950, and even around 1960, with high hopes that are very far from having been realized in 1972. In no part of the field have the discoveries made so far produced the major impact that was then promised. (Lighthill, 1973, pp. 8-9)

Not only did the pessimistic view expressed in the report affect AI community but it also caused turmoil among the public (Lighthill Debate, 1973), which in turn provoked the AI winter (cf. Agar, 2020).

After the first winter, which lasted for about 10 years, a spring arrived, and cherry blossoms bloomed on AI trees in the early 1980s. This burgeoning season lasted for the next 10 years, until the late 1980s. During this period, AI trees attracted bees of AI researchers, butterflies of AI industries, and the honey of AI financial investment from around the world (Anyoha, 2017; Crick, 1995, pp. 182-199; Fetch.ai, 2024b; Partridge, 1987). All three components in the AI ecosystem functioned perfectly, rolling like three cogwheels. The succinct phrases that could summarize the booming 1980s are: (1) a breakthrough in AI programming architecture through a neural network model (cf. Bostrom, 2014, pp. 6-14; Crick, 1995, pp. 182-190; Fridman, 2020; Hopfield, 1982; Rumelhart, Hinton, & Williams, 1986); (2) not general but specific, that is, focusing on "[AI programs] designed to emulate human expertise in specific domains," which became "a staple in corporations worldwide" (Fetch.ai,

2024b).

The breakthrough in the early 1980s was achieved through a new network model for machine learning developed by J. Hopfield, known among AI researchers as the Hopfield network (Hopfield, 1982)[15]. Crick (1995) eloquently articulated the significance of the Hopfield network and its underlying mechanism.

> [After the harsh criticism of the Perceptron by Minsky and Papert] the next development to attract widespread attention came from John Hopfield ⋯ In 1982, he proposed a network now known as a Hopfield network. This was a simple network that fed back on itself. Each of its units[16] could have only two outputs: −1 (inhibition) or +1 (excitation).[17] But each unit had a number of inputs. ⋯ Sometimes ⋯ the unit changed its output, because some of the other units had changed their inputs to it. ⋯ Hopfield was able to show theoretically that, given a set of weights (the strengths of the connections) and any input, the network would neither wander indefinitely nor oscillate but would

15 John Hopfield is "[an American] physicist turned molecular biologist turned brain theorist" (Crick, 1995, p. 182). He has been awarded the 2024 Nobel Prize in Physics in recognition of his pioneering contributions to the development of the Hopfield network. Francis Crick (1916-2004) was a Nobel Prize winner in 1962 with James Watson and Maurice Wilkins for discovering the structure of DNA; Crick was 'a British physicist turned molecular biologist turned neuroscientist' (cf. The Francis Crick Institute, n.d.). For further information about Hopfield and the network in his own voice, see Fridman (2020).

16 The unit indicates "a very oversimplified version of a neuron" (Crick, 1995, p. 183).

17 The terms 'inhibition' and 'excitation' are not arbitrarily chosen in order to contrast the numbers −1 and +1; instead, they are actual physiological terms used by neuroscientists to explain brain function (Kandel, Barres, & Hudspeth, 2013, pp. 212-221). Thus, it is appropriate to understand that the two contrasting numbers serve as numerical signals indicating the actual functions of brain neurons: *inhibition* and *excitation*, respectively.

> quickly reach a stable state. Hopfield's arguments were cogent, and forcibly and clearly written. His network had an enormous appeal to mathematicians and physicists, who felt at last that here was an idea about the brain to which they could relate. The fact that the network was grossly unbiological in many of its details did not worry them all. (p. 182)

Crick's elucidation enables us, including those who are not AI professionals, to sense a wind of change in AI development from both theoretical and computer engineering perspectives. Moreover, although he described the details of the network model as technically "unbiological," its underlying mechanism – processing input and producing output – resembled that of human brains. This is corroborated by Hopfield's own words in his paper:

> Given the dynamical electrochemical properties of neurons and their interconnections (synapses), we readily understand schemes that use a few neurons to obtain elementary useful biological behavior. Our understanding of such simple circuits in electronics allows us to plan larger and more complex circuits which are essential to large computers. Because evolution has no such plan, it becomes relevant to ask whether the ability of large collections of neurons to perform "computational" tasks may in part be a spontaneous collective consequence of having a large number of interacting simple neurons. In physical systems made from a large number of simple elements, interactions among large numbers of elementary components yield collective phenomena such as the stable magnetic orientations and domains in a magnetic system or the vortex patterns in fluid flow. Do analogous collective phenomena in a system of simple interacting neurons

> have useful "computational" correlates? For example, are the stability of memories, the construction of categories of generalization, or time-sequential memory also emergent properties and collective in origin? (Hopfield, 1982, p. 2554, quotation marks in original)[18]

In addition to Hopfield's achievements, the developments made by G. Hinton and his colleagues marked a critical milestone in AI history, ultimately contributing to the creation of recent generative AI, including ChatGPT (cf. Rumelhart, Hinton, & Williams, 1986).[19]

Much like a baby is said to be delivered by storks, ChatGPT was delivered not by creatures with two legs and long beaks but by individuals with two legs and great minds in the AI field. Since then, Hinton has been known as the "Godfather of AI" around the world (60 Minutes, 2023a; BBC News, 2023; CBS Mornings, 2023a).[20] The achievements of Hinton and his

---

18 Although the paper is technically demanding, its introductory paragraphs help those outside the AI field get a sense of how a machine can resemble a human being.

19 The earlier work by Hinton and his colleagues was published in 1981. "While this was read by people working on [artificial] neural networks, it did not have the wide impact of the later book" (Crick, 1995, p. 186). This later book, commonly referred to as 'the PDP book' among AI researchers. (PDP stands for Parallel Distributed Processing, another key feature by which the human brain processes information, in contrast to the serial processing traditionally used by computers.) The book comprises two volumes (Rumelhart & McClelland, 1986; McClelland & Rumelhart, 1986). Volume 1 is 517 pages long, divided into three parts (Parts I to III), and Volume 2 is 581 pages, also divided into three parts (Parts IV to VI). The entire set consists of 26 chapters, evenly distributed with 13 chapters in each volume, authored by researchers from various disciplines, including mathematics, physics, psychology, biology, neuroscience, computer science. Of the 13 chapters in Volume 1, Hinton contributed to five, serving as the first author on two chapters and co-author on three; in Volume 2, he contributed to one chapter as a co-author. Crick also made a significant contribution, authoring one chapter in Part V of Volume 2.

20 Alongside Hopfield, Hinton has been recognized as a 2024 Nobel laureate in

colleagues in the 1980s are worth examining in a little more detail, as their work is directly relevant to the recent emergence of generative AI variants from a technical perspective and is largely analogous to what happens in the ESL classroom from the perspective of the ESL educator. The former helps to understand the significance of their contributions to the timeline of AI development, and the latter offers insights into how similar AI and students are in the process of learning. Among numerous achievements of Hinton and his colleagues is the concept of *backpropagation* (Rumelhart, Hinton, & Williams, 1986), which was most prominently formalized for use in artificial neural networks (cf. Crick, 1995, pp. 187-191; LeCun, Bengio, & Hinton, 2015; Prince, 2023, pp. 203-204; Russell & Norvig, 2021, p. 772). Two key aspects of backpropagation are its *recursive* nature and how it *adapts* to improve performance.[21]

The term 'recursive' in the context of backpropagation in the artificial neural networks can be metaphorically explained using ESL researchers revisiting the ESL classroom.[22] Suppose that ESL

Physics for his seminal contributions to the foundational theories underpinning modern advancements in AI.

21 In many AI textbooks, the concept of *backpropagation* is introduced and explained. The material is usually mathematically demanding, which is understandable since these books are aimed at those studying AI or computer science (Aggarwal, 2023; Bishop & Bishop, 2023; Prince, 2023; Russell & Norvig, 2021). Even for those who seek only a rudimentary understanding of backpropagation, a basic knowledge of calculus is necessary, as the concept inherently involves the notion of *Gradient Descent* in calculus. Given this, Crick (1995, pp. 177-199) explained a series of concepts related to AI development in relatively plain language, which helps non-AI professionals understand their meanings and processes.

22 As A. Korzybski famously stated, "The map is not the territory." It is well acknowledged that, as an ESL professional, there must be extreme caution in using metaphors to explain technical concepts in the AI field, because a metaphoric explanation,

researchers try to solve a complex language learning problem in the ESL classroom. Initially the researchers gather data and form a theory about what happened. However, as they learn new information about the problem, they might realize that some aspects of their initial theory were incorrect.

In this hypothetical context, the research question in the ESL classroom is like a problem that the neural network is trying to solve, such as recognizing faces in photos or writing sentences grammatically. The researchers' initial theory is like the network's first attempt at solving the problem, using initial guesses at the solution. When the researchers (or network) revisit the ESL classroom (or problem), they look back over the data (previous calculations), see where they might have gone wrong, and adjust their theory (update the solution). This revisiting and adjusting happen repeatedly, refining the theory (the solution) until it aligns closely with the reality of the data.

Similarly, in backpropagation, the neural network revisits its own calculations. If the outcome is not as expected, it recursively goes back through the multiple calculations of the network (technically referred to as 'through the layers of the network'), tweaking and adjusting its outcomes (technically, as 'adjusting its parameters') slightly each time to improve the accuracy of the results. This process continues until the network's output matches the expected results as closely as possible (cf. Prince, 2023, pp. 203-204).

---

or model, by its nature, cannot fully capture the numerous subtleties inherent in such concepts. "In spite of all this, I believe that the model is a useful and indeed unescapable tool of thought, in that it enables us to think about the unfamiliar in terms of the familiar" (Bridgman, 1927, p. 53).

Crick (1995) demonstrated the backpropagation more directly by using an educational analogy.

> "[the artificial neural network's] unsupervised learning[23] has a powerful appeal because, in a sense, the network teaches itself. Theorists have devised more powerful learning rules, but these need a "teacher" to tell the network whether it made a good, poor, or bad response to some inputs. ⋯ To train a network it is necessary to have a set of inputs to train it on. ⋯ This is known as the "training set." To be useful it must be a fair sample of the inputs the network is likely to encounter after it has been trained. Usually, the signals of the training set must be fed in several times, so that a lot of training is often required before the network has learned to perform well. This is partly because such networks tend to be set up with random connections. The initial connections in the brain, being controlled to some extent by genetic mechanisms, are usually not completely random. How is the network trained? A signal from the training set is fed

---

23 "Machine learning methods can coarsely be divided into three areas: supervised, unsupervised, and reinforcement learning" (Prince, 2023, p.11). Not surprisingly, a detailed description of each learning method necessarily involves statistical concepts and terms (cf. Aggarwal, 2023, pp.74-96; Bishop & Biship, 2023, pp. 188-189; Prince, 2023, pp. 11-28; Russell & Norvig, 2021, pp. 776-781). What is noteworthy is that the names of the methods are all commonly used in the field of education. To a large extent, this helps to provide a general understanding of each learning method by translating the educational meaning of each name into machine learning terms: in supervised learning, examples and guidance are provided to the artificial neural network; in unsupervised learning, only materials are provided without examples or guidance; in reinforcement learning, rewards or punishments are given. For ESL educators, supervised learning can be analogous to 'explicit learning' in grammar or vocabulary instruction, and unsupervised learning to 'implicit learning.' For a more succinct explanation of the machine learning methods, see Shah (2023, pp. 17-20). Also, see Bishop and Bishop (2023, pp. 188-189) for a brief history of the methods.

> into the network and the network produces an output. This means that the output neurons are each in a special state of activity. The teacher then signals to each output unit what its error is – that is, how its activity differs from the correct one. The difference – between the real activity and the desired one ⋯ Backpropagation is a special example of a learning algorithm requiring a teacher." (pp. 187-188, quotation marks in original)

We can observe fish moving through swim goggles underwater, from which we come to learn how they move. Likewise, Crick's description helps us clearly see how inputs and outputs are processed within the artificial neural network, through which it achieves learning. The description may also, to a large extent, remind ESL educators of the interactions between a teacher and students in the CLT (Communicative Language Teaching) classroom, where students learn through *negotiation of meaning* in multiple interactions (Long, 1983a, 1983b).

In addition to the theoretical advancements in designing AI algorithms, AI researchers have applied them to create a specific type of computer program capable of simulating the decision-making ability of a human expert. This movement, during the late 1970s and the 1980s, is referred to as *Expert Systems* in the AI field (cf. Bostrom, 2014, pp. 17-20; Brown & O'Leary, 1994; Fetch.ai, 2024b; Partridge, 1987; Russell, 2019, pp. 3-6; Russell & Norvig, 2021, pp. 22-24). Expert Systems leverage rule-based reasoning to solve complex problems in specialized domains such as medical diagnosis, engineering, and finance. These systems consist of accumulated empirical knowledge and an inference engine, which applies logical rules to the empirical knowledge to deduce new information and make decisions.

Among the many Expert Systems developed in the 1980s was Dendral, created at Stanford University to assist chemists in identifying unknown organic molecules by analyzing their mass spectra data.[24]

With the updraft of advancing theories in algorithms and computers demonstrating high-level performance in specialized areas, significant investments were made in the AI field by both governments and business corporations, each eager to capitalize on the emerging technologies (cf. IBM, 2024; Novak, 2013; Strategic Computing Initiative, 2023). The surge in investment was driven by the promise of AI to automate complex tasks, enhance data analysis capabilities, and create new efficiencies in operational processes. The influx of funding and the achievements highlighted earlier contributed to the rise of more advanced AI developments.[25]

The atmosphere of the 1980s was upbeat, and everything looked promising, which led to extravagant expectations from both AI researchers and the public regarding upcoming AI developments. The heightened expectations were reasonable, yet another winter storm in the 1990s battered AI communities, which might or might not have been as severe as the one they endured twenty years earlier.[26] While there could be several

---

24 For further details about the Dendral Project, see https://exhibits.stanford.edu/ai/catalog?f%5Btopic_facet%5D%5B%5D=DENDRAL

25 Another indicator of the societal atmosphere in the 1980s was the prominence of personal computers. *Time* magazine underscored this trend with its 1983 cover title, "Machine of the Year: The Computer Moves In" (Time, 1983).

26 "By the mid-1980s, I had become a professor at Berkley, and AI was experiencing a huge revival thanks to the commercial potential of so-called expert systems. The second AI bubble burst when these systems proved to be inadequate for many of the tasks to which

reasons for the second AI winter, they essentially boil down to a substantial disparity between expectations and practical developments (cf. Fetch.ai, 2024c; Glover, 2023; Russell, 2019, p. 4). Although expert systems exhibited high-quality performance, some of the major goals of AI research, such as natural language processing, machine translation, and general problem-solving, proved to be more complex than initially anticipated. The computer engineering techniques and algorithms available at the time were insufficient to solve these problems effectively, leading to disappointment among stakeholders. As the gap between expectations and reality became apparent, both private and public funding sources became disillusioned with AI's slow progress and reduced their financial support.

The second AI winter, like the first, eventually passed, and the field entered the 21st century, characterized by the era of the internet, big data, and remarkable advances in digital technology (60 Minutes, 2023b, 2024; Russell & Norvig, 2021, pp. 26-30). Although the AI field has experienced numerous ups and downs since Turing (1950), "the seeds of today's progress were sown during that AI winter, including early work on large-scale probabilistic reasoning systems and what later became known as *deep learning*" (Russell, 2019, p. 6, italic in original). Despite two harsh winters, the *stream of artificial consciousness*[27]– the

---

they were applied. Again, the machines just weren't smart enough. An AI winter ensued. My own AI course at Berkley, currently bursting with over nine hundred students, had just twenty-five students in 1990" (Russell, 2019, p. 4).

27 The term is inspired by the notion of *stream of consciousness*, originally proposed by James (1950/1890). "Consciousness, then, does not appear to itself chopped up in bits. Such words as 'chain' or train' do not describe it fitly as it presents itself in the first instance. It is nothing jointed; it flows. A 'river' or a 'stream' are the metaphors by which

pertinacious endeavor by AI researchers to computationally create machines that can think and process emotions like the human mind – has not been interrupted but has instead tenaciously continued through the thread of the relentless efforts of AI researchers. Around 2011, phenomenal advancements were made in speech recognition, visual recognition, and machine translation in the field of AI, thanks to deep learning (cf. Bengio, LeCun, & Hinton, 2021; Krizhevsky, Sutskever, & Hinton, 2017; LeCun, Bengio, & Hinton, 2015; Russell & Norvig, 2021, p. 26-27). This has ushered us into another booming period of AI – the age of the "Cambrian explosion"[28] – allowing

---

it is most naturally described. *In talking of it hereafter, let us call it the stream of thought, of consciousness, or of subjective life*" (James, 1950, p. 239, quotation marks and italic in original). The notion, stream of consciousness, is used in the modern novel as a narrative technique that depicts the continuous flow of a character's thoughts, feelings, and perceptions as they occur, often in a disjointed or nonlinear fashion (cf. Holman, Hibbard, & Thrall, 1979).

28 In the AI community, researchers figuratively refer to the recent AI boom as "Cambrian explosion" (e.g., Aggarwal, 2023, p. 3; Li, 2023, p. 207). "Half a billion years after the emergence of biological vision led to the Cambrian explosion beneath the waves of an ancient ocean, it was hard not to wonder if we were on the verge of a similar inflection point. Would the advent of machine vision trigger a new avalanche of evolution, this time in a digital form?" (Li, 2023, p. 207) In earth science, the Cambrian explosion is "one of the major evolutionary transitions in the history of life. ⋯ during a relatively narrow time span in the early Cambrian (after about 542 [million years ago]), there is an explosive appearance of many different, morphologically distinctive fossils, including representatives of most of the major animal groups that are alive today" (Ervin & Valentine, 2013, p. v). As stated in the introductory remarks by Ervin and Valentine (2013), the Cambrian period, which occurred around 540 to 480 million years ago, is a time in Earth's history when there was an explosion of diverse and complex life forms, including the first appearance of many major groups of animals (cf. Steven & Luczaj, 2014, pp. 301-311). Similarly, it might be said in the future that *the artificial Cambrian explosion*, which occurred around 2022 and 2023, is a time in AI's history when there was an explosion of diverse and complex AI forms, including the first appearance of many major groups of generative AIs. In fact, since the end of 2022, numerous major tech companies, including OpenAI, Google, Microsoft,

us to experience the marvels of ChatGPT and other generative AI variants (Paul G. Allen School, 2024; Wolfram, 2023).

Meta, and Apple, have unveiled scores of generative AIs within just a year (cf. Apple Machine Learning Research, 2024; Castellan, 2024; Heikkilä, 2024e; Meta, 2024; O'Donnell, 2024; OpenAI, 2024b).

Chapter 2

Innerspace[29]

Lt. Tuck Pendleton: I'm right here, INSIDE you INSIDE YOUR BODY!
Jack Putter: [stands up] Oh God! Somebody help me! I'M POSSESSED!
...
Lt. Tuck Pendleton: Alright. Jack, my name is Lt. Tuck Pendleton. I've been miniaturised. I was supposed to be injected into the body of a laboratory rabbit and somehow I got inside you instead.
Jack Putter: What do you mean somehow? How?
Lt. Tuck Pendleton: All I know is I was inside a syringe, and now I'm inside you.

(Dante, 1987)[30]

29 The title originates from Dante (1987).
30 The transcript is from https://www.imdb.com/title/tt0093260/quotes/?item=qt0482277

Swans on a lake appear serene, yet beneath the water, they are busy paddling hard to maintain their serenity. Similarly, although the outcomes from ChatGPT may seem to come easily, the underlying artificial neural networks are engaged in rapid and intricate processes (cf. Wolfram, 2023, pp. 60-91). The same is true for our brains. When we see a cat and simply say "a cat," our brains are actively processing this 'cat' information through a swift and convoluted mechanism (Abbott, Losonczy, & Sawtell, 2021, pp. 103-104; Corbett & Chen, 2017, p. 288; Crick, 1995, pp. 121-159).

As an ESL professional and merely a consumer of generative AI, it is acceptable to use it for simple, straightforward outcomes; however, as an ESL professional and a pedagogical user of generative AI, it is far more beneficial to understand the underlying principles behind the apparent outcomes. This not only helps in using generative AI as a teaching or research aid but also deepens our understanding of it.[31] Similar to ESL educators in reading programs, who are not satisfied with simply knowing a learner's level of reading proficiency, they thus aim to probe into the cognitive processes occurring within the learner's mind during reading. These coveted insights are provided by L2 reading process models, knowledge of which significantly helps

---

31 The benefits of understanding how ChatGPT works are well described in Hinton's statement: "That was the first language model to be trained with backpropagation [in 1985]. And it was really, you can think of it as the ancestor of these big models now. And I'm going to talk about it in some detail, because it's so small and simple that you can actually understand something about how it works. And once you understand how that works, it gives you insight into what's going on in these bigger models." (University of Oxford, 2024, 6:52-7:15).

to enhance ESL teachers' instructional strategies and enrich their understanding of how learners read and interpret text in the target language (Carrell, Devine, & Eskey, 1998; Grabe, 2009; Grabe & Stoller, 2002).

ChatGPT and other generative AI variants operate using algorithms designed around artificial neural networks (cf. Aggarwal, 2023; Prince, 2023; Wolfram, 2023). Decades ago, when ordinary people encountered the term 'neural networks' in everyday life, it was more likely to be associated with the human brain rather than with anything related to computers. Now, however, it is necessary to consider the context to properly understand whether the term refers to artificial or biological neurons. As the name suggests, artificial neural networks are both theoretical and conceptual replicas, or models, of human neural networks (Bishop & Bishop, 2023, pp. 16-17; Buduma, Buduma, & Papa, 2022, pp. 76-77; Shadlen & Kandel, 2021; Russell & Norvig, 2021, pp. 11-12). Although it may seem natural and unsurprising that artificial and biological neural networks are alike,[32] it is astonishing to see how closely artificial neural networks resemble those in the human brain, especially to the eye of the ESL educator (cf. McClelland, Rumelhart, & Hinton, 1986; Seung & Yuste, 2013).

---

32 Given the history of science, it seems natural and unsurprising, much like "[w]hen humanity wanted to understand flight, we garnered our first inspiration from birds; when George de Mestral invented Velcro, he got the idea from burdock fruits; when Benjamin Franklin sought to explore electricity, his first sparks of understanding came from lightning. Nature has, throughout the history of human innovation, long been a wondrous guide. Nature also offers us clues as to how intelligence works – the clearest locus of which is, of course, the human brain" (Bennett, 2023, pp. 3-4).

The human brain processes information from the outside (e.g., eyes, skin, or tongue) through interconnected neurons (Abbott, Losonczy, & Sawtell, 2021, pp. 103-104). Artificial neurons, replicated from those in our brain, are represented as small circles in almost every textbook or reference material on AI (e.g., Aggarwal, 2023; Bishop & Bishop, 2023; Buduma, Buduma, & Papa, 2022; Prince, 2023). Because the artificial neurons are symbolized as circles in AI materials, we might figuratively imagine that neurons in our brain look like minuscule circles. They are, however, much more than we might imagine.[33] Neurons in our brain are technically explained by scholars in the field of neuroscience as follows:

> Individual nerve cells, or neurons, are the basic signaling units of the brain. The human brain contains a huge number of these cells, on the order of 86 billion neurons, that can be classified into at least a thousand different types. Yet this great variety of neurons is less of a factor in the complexity of human behavior than is their organization into anatomical circuits with precise functions. Indeed, one key organizational principle of the brain is that nerve cells with *similar* properties can produce different actions because of the way they are interconnected. Because relatively few principles of organization of the nervous system give rise to considerable functional complexity, it is possible to learn a great deal about how the nervous system produces behavior by focusing on five basic features of the

33 "Parts of what makes the nervous systems so distinctive is how distinctive neurons are as cells. Cells are usually small, self-contained entities – consider little round red blood cells: Neurons, in contrast, are highly asymmetrical, elongated beasts, typically with processes sticking out all over the place" (Sapolsky, 2017, p. 680).

> nervous system:
> 1. The structural components of individual nerve cells;
> 2. The mechanisms by which neurons produce signals within themselves and between each other;
> 3. The patterns of connection between nerve cells and between nerve cells and their targets (muscle and gland effectors);
> 4. The relationship of different patterns of interconnection to different types of behavior; and
> 5. How neurons and their connections are modified by experience
>
> (Shadlen & Kandel, 2021, p. 56, italic in original)

For a better understanding of the artificial neural networks in relation to the brain neurons, three key features mentioned above are notable. They are (1) "the basic signaling units of the brain," (2) "a huge number of neurons" beyond our arithmetic capabilities, and (3) "the way neurons are interconnected." To clarify, although there are many different types of neurons in the human brain, the way these neurons are arranged and connected to each other is more important for explaining complex human behaviors. It is not just the variety of neurons that matters, but more importantly, how they are organized into specific pathways and networks that perform detailed functions.[34]

In less technical terms, the brain neurons are described from the perspective of a professional in the AI industry, which

34 For further information on the brain neurons, see Abbott, Losonczy, and Sawtell (2021, pp. 101-104), Crick (1995, pp. 91-105), Sapolsky (2017, pp.679-693), and Shadlen and Kandel (2021, pp. 56-57, 61-67).

still clarifies the aspects congruent with those highlighted in the technical description: the number of neurons, their interconnections, and the complexity of these interconnections.

> The human brain contains eighty-six billion neurons and over a hundred trillion connections. Each of those connections is so minuscule – less than thirty nanometers wide[35] – that they can barely be seen under even the most powerful microscopes. These connections are bunched together in a tangled mess – within a single cubic millimeter (the width of a single letter on penny), there are over *one billion* connections. But, the sheer number of connections is only one aspect of what makes the brain complex; even if we mapped the wiring of each neuron we would still be far from understanding how the brain works. Unlike the electrical connections in your computer, where wires all communicate using the same signal – electrons – across each of the neural connections, hundreds of different chemicals are passed, each with completely different effects. The simple fact that two neurons connect to each other tells us little about what they are communicating. And worst of all, these connections themselves are in a constant state of change, with some neurons branching out and forming new connections, while others are retracting and removing old ones. Altogether, this makes reverse engineering how the brain works an ungodly task. (Bennett, 2023, p. 4, italic in original)

35 The term, 'nano,' denotes a factor of 10^{-9}. Thus, one nanometer measures 10^{-9}meters, which is equivalent to 10^{-11}centimeters or 10^{-12}millimeters. Human hair diameters typically range from 17 and 181 micrometers (B10NUMB3R5, n.d.), with 'micro' representing 10^{-6}. Considering the size of both neural connections and a strand of human hair, the width of the largest neural connections is 30×10^{-9}meters, whereas the thinnest hairs are 17×10^{-6}meters. Thus, neural connections are about 600 times smaller than the thinnest hair, highlighting the neuron's minuscule size.

From a slightly different angle, the brain neurons are concisely outlined in a reference book on machine learning for aspiring AI developers in a short and clear-cut fashion. The focus remains on the number, the connections, and the connectional complexity.

> The foundational unit of the human brain is the neuron. A tiny piece of the brain, about the size of grain of rice, contains over 10,000 neurons, each of which forms an average of 6,000 connections with other neurons. It's this massive biological network that enables us to experience the world around us. Our goal in this section is to use this this natural structure to build machine learning models that solve problems in an analogous way. (Buduma, Buduma, & Papa, 2022, p. 76)

The three verbal explanations of the brain neurons are much more accessible with the help of visual aids. While the verbal explanations help us understand neurons holistically, the visual ones provide us with a snapshot of an individual neuron. By 'snapshot,' this indicates that only a single neuron is depicted, rather than the entire network of the brain neurons. Figure 2 presents the brain neurons as illustrated in reference materials in the fields of neuroscience and AI. Specifically, Figure 2-A is derived from the field of neuroscience, while Figures 2-B and 2-C are from those in the field of deep learning.

In Figure 2-A, information from the external environment enters a neuron through the dendrites (shown on the left side of the figure) and travels to the cell body (at the center of the figure). From there, it is transferred along the axon to another neuron (depicted in gray on the right side of the figure).

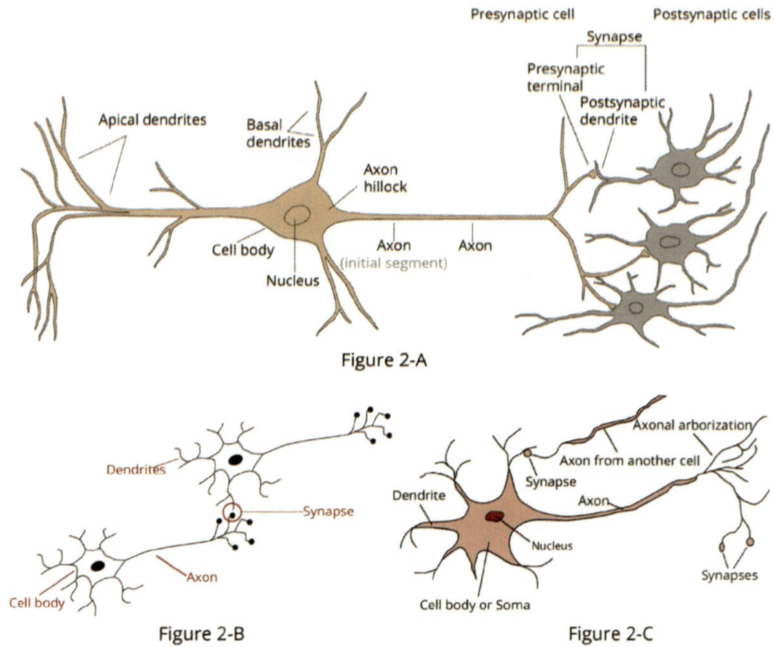

Figure 2. Graphical presentation of a neuron from reference materials in neuroscience and AI:Figure 2-A is replicated and adapted from Shadlen and Kandel (2021, p. 57)[36]; Figure 2-B replicated from Bishop and Bishop (2023, p. 16); Figure 2-C replicated from Russell and Norvig (2021, p. 12)

Between the yellow-colored neuron and the gray-colored neuron, there is a microscopic gap known as a synapse, through which information is transmitted from one neuron to another.[37] This neural transmission process is well elucidated with regard to human behavior by Shadlen and Kandel (2021), as follows.

> Every behavior is mediated by specific sets of interconnected neurons, and every neuron's behavioral function is determined by its connections with other neurons. A simple behavior, the knee-jerk reflex, will illustrate this. ⋯ The stretching of just one muscle, the quadriceps, activates several hundred sensory neurons, each of which makes direct contact with 45 to 50 motor neurons. This pattern of connection, in which one neuron activates many target cells, is called *divergence*. It is especially common in the input stages of the nervous system; by distributing its signals to many target cells, a single neuron can exert wide

---

36 The original figure is presented in portrait orientation, and Figure 2-A is replicated and adapted in landscape orientation for this book. Figure 2-A shows "[t]he structure of a neuron. Most neurons in the vertebrate nervous system have several main features in common. The cell body contains the nucleus, the storehouse of genetic information, and gives rise to two types of cell processes: axons and dendrites" (Shadlen & Kandel, 2021, p. 57).

37 For a reference on how researchers in the field of child cognitive development explain synapses and neurons, see Nelson III, Thomas, and Haan (2006, p. 11): "Synapses generally refer to the point of contact between two neurons. Depending on the receiving neuron, the resulting action can be excitatory (promoting an action potential) or inhibitory (reducing the likelihood of an action potential)." For a succinct explanation of "synapses and learning" along with visual graphics, see Eagleman (2015, p. 82): "As synapses change their potency, information flows through the network differently. If a connection gets weak enough, it withers and goes away. If it gets strengthened, it can sprout new connections. Some of this reconfiguring is guided by reward systems. ⋯ Austin's brain networks have been reshaped – very slowly, very subtly – by the success or failure of each attempted move, over hundreds of hours of practice."

> and diverse influence. Conversely, a single motor cell in the knee-jerk circuit receives 200 to 450 input contacts from approximately 130 sensory cells. This pattern of connection is called *convergence*. It is common at the output stages of the nervous system; a target motor cell that receives information from many sensory neurons is able to integrate information from many sources. Each sensory neuron input produces relatively weak excitation, so convergence also ensures that a motor neuron is activated only when a sufficient number of sensory neurons are activated together.
>
> (pp. 61-63, italic in original)

The schematic elucidation presented by Shadlen and Kandel (2021) delineates key features of information flow and associated mechanisms as applied in the domains of artificial neural networks and deep learning. The explanation encompasses the transmission of data from one neuron to another, with a particular focus on the interconnections between them. Initially, the process involves an expansion from a singular neuron to an array of multiple neurons, which subsequently condenses into a fewer number of neurons. Sapolsky (2017) explains this by focusing on the function of neurons, adopting the style of a storytime host, which reminds ESL educators of a conversation among a teacher, learners, and between learners themselves.

> What neurons do is talk to one another, cause one another to get excited. At one end of a neuron are its metaphorical ears, specialized processes that receive information from another neuron. At the other end are the processes that are the mouth, that communicate with the next neuron in line. The ears, the inputs, are called dendrites. The output begins with a single long cable called an axon, which then

> ramifies into axonal endings – these axon terminals are the mouths ⋯ Those axon terminals connect to the dendrites of the next neuron in line. Thus a neuron's dendritic ears are informed that the neuron behind it is excited. The flow of information then sweeps from the dendrites to the cell body to the axon to the axon terminals, and is then passed to the next neuron. (Sapolsky, 2017, p. 681)

His explanation can help us feel as if we are traveling inside a neuron via a virtual *Nano Capsule Submarine* to see what is happening within. The points echo those in Shadlen and Kandel (2021). Continuing, he examines the neuron more closely, putting a magnifying glass to the dendrites and axons to explore the nature of the information inside.

> Let's translate "flow of information" into quasi chemistry. What actually goes from the dendrites to the axon terminals? A wave of electrical excitation. Inside the neuron are various positively and negatively charged ions. Just outside the neuron's membrane are other positively and negatively charged ions. When a neuron has gotten an exciting signal from the previous neuron at the end of one single dendritic fiber, channels in the membrane in that dendrite open, allowing various ions to flow in and others to flow out, and the net result is that the inside of the end of that dendrite becomes more positively charged. The charge spreads toward the axon terminal, where it is passed to the next neuron. ⋯ when a neuron has gotten a hugely excitatory message from the previous neuron in line, its insides can become positively charged relative to the extracellular space around it ⋯ the neuron now has something to say and it is screaming its head off. What might things look like then when the neuron has nothing to say, has not been stimulated? Maybe ⋯ neutral charges? No, never! ⋯ neurons are all about contrasts. When a neuron has nothing to say, ⋯ the inside of

> the neuron is *negatively* charged relative to the outside. You couldn't ask for a more dramatic contrast[38]: I have nothing to say = inside of the neuron is negatively charged. I have something to say = inside is positive. No neuron ever confuses the two. (Sapolsky, 2017, p. 682, quotation marks and italic in original)

While both the verbal explanations and the snapshot-like figures effectively illustrate the processes and functions of neurons, researchers in the fields of neuroscience and machine learning employ simpler graphical models designed to reflect key aspects of brain neurons. In Figure 3, Sapolsky (2017) uses a skeleton-X-ray-like model consisting only of circles, lines (straight or curved), and wishbone symbols, to portray these aspects. The circles represent neurons, and the lines indicate connections among them. Figure 4 presents a graphical model of the artificial neural networks used in deep learning (Bishop & Bishop, 2023; Prince, 2023), where each circle represents a unit signal (equivalent to a neuron) and the lines represent connections. Although Sapolsky's model appears simple, as he notes, "a neuron, two neurons, a neuronal circuit. We are ready now, as a last step, to scale up to the level of thousands of neurons at once" (Sapolsky, 2017, p. 702). Thus, the meaning

---

38 In the prior chapter, Crick's (1995, p. 182) discussion of the Hopfield network examined two contrasting numerical signals, -1 and +1, representing *inhibition* and *excitation*, respectively. These numerical signals effectively illustrate "the dramatic contrast" – negatively charged (inhibition) with minus and positively charged (excitation) with plus. The two numbers are perfectly coded as simple and contrasting, -1 vs. +1, rather than -1 vs. +2 or -2 vs. +1.

within the two models in Figures 3 and 4 is fundamentally alike.

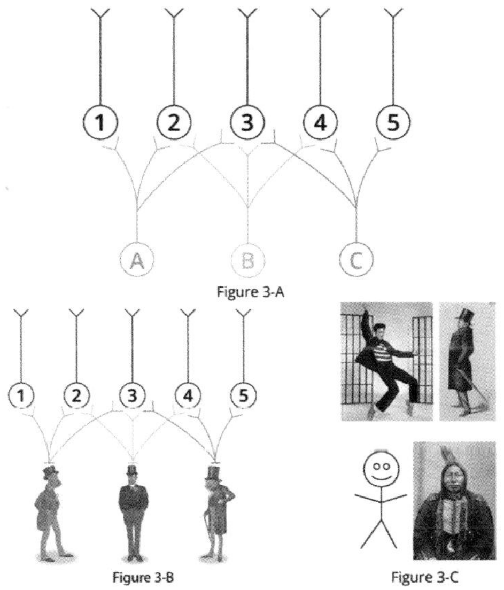

Figure 3. Simple graphical models reflecting brain neurons: Figure 3-A and 3-B are replicated from Sapolsky (2017, pp. 700-701); Figure 3-C is replicated and adapted from Sapolsky (2017, p. 701)

Using a hypothetical example, Sapolsky's (2017) model in Figure 3 explicitly demonstrates how critical neural connections are when confronting a new problem that requires knowledge to solve.

> "[In Figure 3-A] Neuron A projects to neurons 1, 2, and 3; neuron B projects to 2, 3, and 4, etc. Now let's show how hypothetical this circuit is by giving neurons A, B, and C completely imaginary functions. [In Figure 3-B] Neuron A responds to the picture of the guy on the left, B to the guy in the middle, C to the one on the right: What can neuron 1 learn? How to recognize that particular guy. Neuron 5 is equally specialized. But what can neuron 3

> learn? How Victorian gentlemen dressed. It's the neuron that will help you identify the Victorian in the quartet [in Figure 3-C]. Neuron 3's knowledge is general and comes from the overlap of the first layer's projections. Neuron 2 and 4 are also generalist neurons, but they're less accurate because they have only two exemplars each. So neuron 3 is at the convergent center of this network. And the fanciest parts of the brain are wired up in a way that resembles this fairy-tale circuit, writ large – at the same time, neuron 3 is a more peripheral element in some other circuit sending projections to it ··· neuron 1 is at the very center of some other network in the fourth dimension, and so on. All of these neurons are embedded within multiple networks."
>
> (Sapolsky, 2017, pp. 700-701)

Figure 4 displays graphical models of artificial neural networks used in the materials on deep learning. In these materials, the Perceptron (Figure 4-B) is often described as a single-layer model, followed by a multi-layer model (Figure 4-C) that illustrates mechanisms of deep learning.[39] Similar to the model in Figure 3, the symbols in Figure 4 are straightforward: a circle represents a signaling unit (equivalent to a neuron), and an arrow indicates a connection to another unit (equivalent to connections between neurons).[40]

---

39 "The term "deep learning" was first used by Dechter (1986)" (Prince, 2023, p. 96, quotation marks in original). Introducing techniques to enhance the efficiency of search algorithms by incorporating learning processes, Dechter (1986, p. 180) used the contrasting terms, "deep learning" and "shallow learning." For further information about Dechter and her contributions to AI research, see Grattarola (2018).

40 In addition to connecting the units, the arrow lines also indicate the direction of information processing, which is toward where the arrowhead points. Although the meaning of the arrow lines is not technically identical, this may help ESL professionals understand the diagram in Figure 4. For those who have experience with SEM (Structural Equation Modeling)

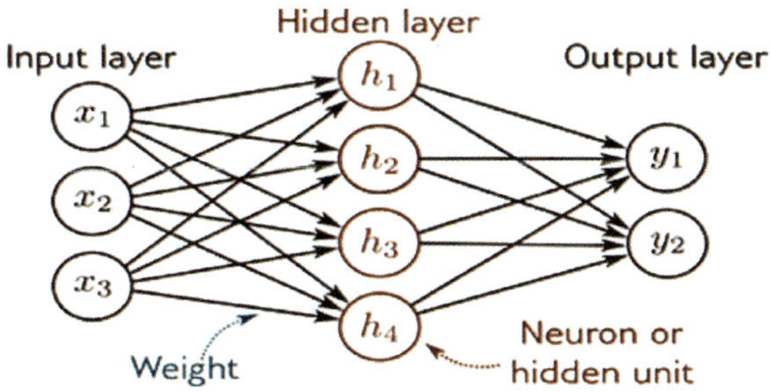

Figure 4-A

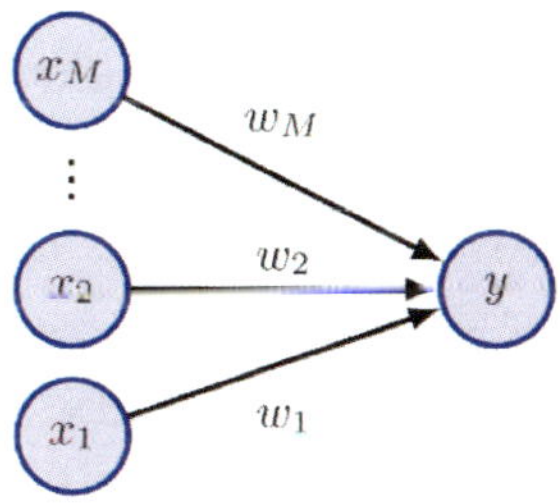

Figure 4-B

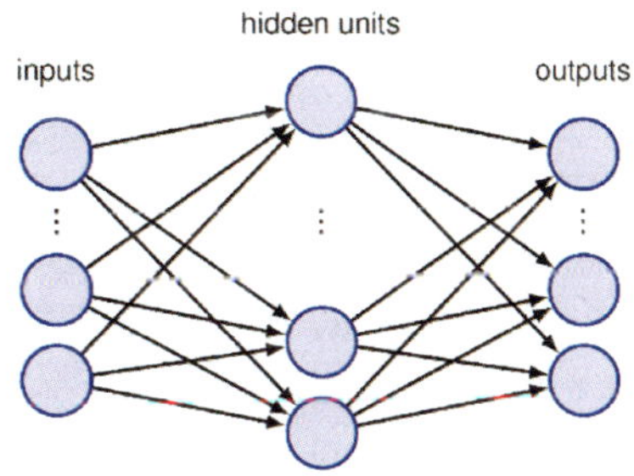

Figure 4-C

Figure 4. Graphical models of artificial neural networks from materials on deep learning: Figure 4-A is replicated from Prince (2023, p. 69); Figure 4-B replicated from Bishop and Bishop (2023, p. 17); and Figure 4-C is replicated from Bishop and Bishop (2023, p. 19).

---

through courses in quantitative research methods or through their own data analysis, the graphical model in Figure 4 closely resembles SEM diagrams that depict relationships between variables. Specifically, the diagrams for multiple regression in the SEM materials look similar to the graphical model of a single-layer network (cf. Schumacker & Lomax, 2010, pp. 125-141). In these diagrams for multiple regression, all independent variables, such as ESL learner's motivation, level of satisfaction with an ESL course, and daily study hours on English (denoted as x1, x2, x3, x4, etc.), are vertically aligned on the left side, each within a rectangular symbol, and each is connected to a dependent variable, such as level of learner's achievement on a proficiency test (denoted as y), with an arrow line that has a rightward-pointing arrowhead (Schumacker & Lomax, 2010, p. 131). Similarly, Figure 4-B shows all inputs vertically aligned on the left side, linked to units in subsequent layers.

As shown in Figure 4, a layer between the 'input layer' (or simply 'input') and the 'output layer' (or simply 'output') is referred to as a *hidden layer* (cf. Aggarwal, 2023, pp. 13-14; Bishop & Bishop, 2023, p. 19).[41] A neural network with no hidden layers is called a single-layer network, or Perceptron.[42] The number of hidden layers can be one or more, depending on the complexity of the network. "For historical reason any neural network with at least one hidden layer is also called a *multi-layer perceptron*" (Prince, 2023, p. 69).[43] Piccinini (2020) encapsulates the key aspects of the entire process within the model shown in Figure 4:

> Neural networks are ensembles of connected signal-processing units ("neurons"). Typically, they have units that receive inputs from the environment (input units), units

---

41 The reason they are referred to as *hidden layers* is "because the units do not connect directly with the world outside the network" (Crick, 1995, p. 189). Cybenko (1989) highlighted the importance of a hidden layer in artificial neural networks. He proved that adding a hidden layer enables artificial neural networks to overcome the major limitations of earlier models like Rosenblatt's Perceptron, which struggled with complex, non-linear problems. Cybenko's contribution laid the groundwork for modern deep learning with multiple hidden layers.

42 Technically, a Perceptron is a type of single-layer neural network, typically used for binary classification tasks (Bishop & Bishop, 2023, pp. 131-134). It consists of a single layer connecting the inputs directly to an output. "The history of artificial neural networks can broadly be divided into three distinct phases according to the level of sophistication of the networks as measured by the number of 'layers' of processing. A simple neural model ... can be viewed as having a single layer of processing corresponding to the single layer of connections ... One of the most important such models in the history of neural computing is the perceptron (Rosenblatt, 1962)" (Bishop & Bishop, 2023, pp. 17-18).

43 "Networks with one hidden layer ··· are sometimes referred to as *shallow neural networks*. Networks with multiple hidden layers ··· are referred to as *deep neural networks*" (Prince, 2023, p. 69).

> that yield outputs to the environment (output units), and units that communicate only with other units in the system (hidden units). Each unit receives input signals and delivers output signals as a function of its input and current state. As a result of their unit's activities and organization, neural networks turn the input received by their input units into the output units. (p. 107, quotation marks in original)

In addition to the similarities between the models in Figures 3 and 4 regarding their representations, there is another noteworthy affinity: how artificial neural networks differ in computations from traditional computers. Two terms are crucial for understanding the difference: *serial processing* and *parallel processing*.[44] To point out, parallel processing is characteristic of artificial neural networks, while serial processing typically describes the method of information processing in many traditional computers (Caulfield, 2009; CNBC, 2023). Given that artificial neural networks resemble the human brain, parallel processing mirrors how our brain actually processes information (McClelland, Rumelhart, & Hinton, 1986).

With regard to contrasting serial processing with parallel processing, a series of four explanations is presented below to facilitate understanding the difference between the two processes and why artificial neural networks employ parallel processing. The explanations are presented in sequence from Crick (1995), Friedenberg (2010), Kandel, Barres, and Hudspeth (2013), and McClelland, Rumelhart, and Hinton (1986). Crick's

44 In fact, the two terms are not novel to ESL professionals, as they are discussed in L2 literature such as Brown (2006, p. 31).

explanation serves as a good opening paragraph about the two processes, balancing the use of terms between computation and neurophysiology. Friedenberg (2010) elaborates on Crick's account, situating it within the framework of "the computational theory of cognition," with a focus on computations (Piccinini, 2020, p. 107). Kandel, Barres, and Hudspeth (2013) explain parallel processing in the language of neuroscience. McClelland, Rumelhart, and Hinton (1986) show what leading AI researchers remarked in their own words during the time when the notion of parallel processing from neuroscience was applied to the development of artificial neural networks.

> ··· the high-speed digital computer, sometimes referred to as the von Neumann[45] computer after the outstanding mathematician who helped bring it to birth. Because computers, like the brain, can manipulate symbols as well as numbers, it is natural to imagine that the brain is some rather complicated form of von Neumann computer. This parallel, if carried too far, leads to unrealistic theories. A computer is built with intrinsically fast components. Even in a PC, the basic cycle, or clock rate, is more than 10 million operations per second. For a neuron, on the other hand, a typical firing rate[46] is in the region of only a

---

45 John von Neumann (1903-1957) was a pioneering mathematician and physicist known for his contributions to a wide range of fields, including the development of game theory, quantum mechanics, and computer science. He is particularly renowned for the von Neumann architecture, a foundational framework for modern computer design (cf. Institute for Advanced Study, n.d.).

46 In neuroscience, 'firing' and 'spikes' are closely related terms (cf. "Action Potential," 2024; Gardner & Johnson, 2013, pp. 1338-1344). 'Firing' refers to the process by which neurons communicate via electrical impulses called action potentials, which occur when a neuron receives a strong enough stimulus to cause a rapid change in electrical charge,

> *hundred* spikes per second. The computer is getting on for a million times faster. A high-speed super-computer ··· is even faster. Largely speaking the operations in a computer are serial – that is, one after another. The arrangements in the brain, on the other hand, are usually massively parallel. For example, about a million axons go from each eye to the brain, *all working simultaneously*. This kind of wiring[47] compensates somewhat for the relatively slow behavior of neurons. It also means that the loss of a few scattered neurons is unlikely to appreciably alter the brain's behavior. In technical jargon, the brain is said to "degrade gracefully." A computer is brittle. Even a little damage to it, or a small error in its program, may cause havoc. A computer can degrade catastrophically. (Crick, 1995, p. 178, italic and quotation marks in original)

The explanation clearly shows the contrasting features of the two processes in the computer and the human brain. It can be summarized in three key highlights. First, as the terms literally indicate, *serial* is "one after another" and *parallel* is "all working simultaneously." Second, the former can be faster than the latter in terms of processing speed, under specific conditions. Third, the consequence of errors in processing is catastrophic in the

leading to the release of chemical signals in synapses to neighboring neurons. This process is essential for brain functions like thought, movement, and sensory processing. And 'spikes' refer to the rapid electrical impulses, also known as action potentials, that neurons generate to communicate with each other. These spikes occur when a neuron's potential quickly rises and falls, transmitting information along the neuron's axon and across synapses to neighboring neurons.

47 "This arrangement of dendrites, axons, and synapses knits your 128 billion individual neurons into a network. To make things simpler, I'll refer to this whole arrangement as the "wiring" of your brain" (Barrett, 2020, p. 30, quotation marks in original).

former (it cannot move on because of 'one after another') while the latter can find another way around to reach the output. In a similar vein, Friedenberg (2010) elaborates on the two processes within the framework of "the computational theory of cognition"[48] through three steps, followed by concise visual descriptions: (1) contrasting the type of processing between the computer and the human brain, (2) speed of each processing, and (3) accuracy in relation to error and consequences. He begins by contrasting *serial* and *parallel processing.*

> The human brain employs a **parallel** processing or distributed computing style, where a task is performed by the simultaneous execution of multiple processors. For example, in human vision, unique aspects of the visual scene are broken down and processed separately by distinct brain regions. One area processes color, another form, and yet another motion. The results of all these computations can then be integrated or evaluated at some later stage. This makes sense when we think of the brain's architecture, which is a network of billions of neurons. Each neuron or collection of neurons can act as a processing element performing some specific task. Separate aspects of a computationally intensive problem like object identification can thus be broken up and assigned to multiple specialized processors. This distributes the workload and accelerates the time it takes to perform the task. Most contemporary computers are **serial processors.** They process information one step at a time. In this type of architecture, one instruction gets carried out before another can begin. The

48 For further discussion of "the computational theory of cognition," see Piccinini (2020, pp. 107-155).

> result of this computation then serves as the input to the next processor and so on in a linear fashion. (Friedenberg, 2010, p. 24, bold in original)

The content covered in the comparisons largely aligns with Crick's (1995, p. 178). Crick elucidates the distinctive features of the two processes, balancing computational terms with physiological terms (e.g., "firing" and "spikes") and technical jargon. In contrast, Friedenberg (2010) describes the differences by drawing comparisons between computers and human brains. This distinction becomes more apparent in the subsequent steps of his description.

> In performing a mathematical operation, a desktop computer would need to execute each step in the process one at a time. Having stated this, it is possible to build parallel processing computers that mimic brain function. … You might think that a parallel processing style would always solve a problem more rapidly. But this isn't always true. For one thing, it depends upon the actual speed of processing. A fast serial processor could solve a problem more quickly than a slow parallel processor. … Computers differ from brains in their accuracy as well as speed. In his classical 1958 paper *The Computer and the Brain*, John von Neumann compares the two. He finds that computers, even those in use nearly half a century ago, can represent and use variable with up to twelve decimal places of accuracy. The neuron is limited to about only two decimal places of accuracy. This is especially troubling for extended computations, because small errors made early on can become magnified in later steps. Perhaps the reason the brain performs its wonders without this kind of accuracy is that it relies primarily on analog representations or on

> nonnumerical symbolic representations. (Friedenberg, 2010, pp. 24-26, italic in original)

Both explanations help us gain an overarching understanding of the key distinctive features of the two processes. The explanations point out (1) the contrasting ways of processing, (2) the comparison of speed between the two processes, and (3) the degree of seriousness caused by errors. These features are much clearer in the two simple and contrasting figures in Figure 5.

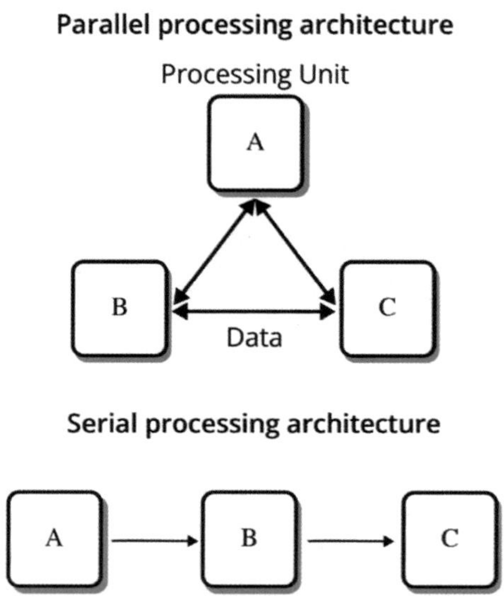

Figure 5. Visual representation of serial processing and parallel processing, replicated from Friedenberg (2010, p. 25)

Along with the two accounts, Kandel, Barres, and Hudspeth (2013) describe the processes in the language of neurophysiology. While they use the language of neuroscience, the beginning of their description helps us understand the three steps of information processing in the brain, which have been discussed earlier in Figures 3 and 4, and draw a mental picture of them: input (i.e., "sensory input"), neurons to neurons (i.e., "intermediate processing"), and output (i.e., "motor output"). These steps are the same as those presented in the earlier two descriptions, and they clearly illustrate the feature of our brain, "degrade gracefully," in contrast to that of the computer, "degrade catastrophically" (Crick, 1995, p. 178).

> Broadly speaking, as we have seen, there are three components of the neural control of behavior: sensory input, intermediate processing, and motor output. In vertebrates each component is likely to be mediated by a single group or several distinct groups of neurons. Moreover, each component may have multiple neural pathways that simultaneously provide the same or similar information. The deployment of several neuronal groups or pathways to convey similar information is called *parallel processing*. Parallel processing also occurs in a single pathway when different neurons in the pathway perform similar computations simultaneously. Parallel processing makes enormous sense as an evolutionary strategy for building a more powerful brain, for it increases both the speed and reliability of function within the central nervous system. The importance of abundant, highly specific parallel connections has long been recognized by scientists attempting to construct theoretical models of the brain. The branch of computer science known as artificial intelligence originally used serial processing to simulate the brain's cognitive processes – pattern recognition, learning, memory, and motor performance. These serial models performed many tasks rather well, including playing chess. However, they performed poorly with other computations

> that the brain does almost instantaneously, such as recognizing faces or comprehending speech. (Kandel, Barres, & Hudspeth, 2013, pp. 231-233, italic in original)

To integrate the three explanations regarding the differences between the computer and the human brain in information processing, the following excerpt is from the opening chapter of the PDP book (McClelland, Rumelhart, & Hinton, 1986), which is based on the features of parallel processing in the human brain. The excerpt can immerse us in a live discussion, presenting the voices of leading AI scholars as they discuss the application of parallel processing in developing artificial neural networks:

> What makes people smarter than machines? They certainly are not quicker or more precise. Yet people are far better at perceiving objects in natural scenes and noting their relations, at understanding language and retrieving contextually appropriate information from memory, ··· In our view, people are smarter than today's computers because the brain employs a basic computational architecture that is more suited to deal with a central aspect of the natural information processing tasks that people are so good at. ··· we will show through examples that these tasks generally require the simultaneous consideration of many pieces of information or constraints. Each constraint may be imperfectly specified and ambiguous, yet each can play a potentially decisive role in determining the outcome of processing. (McClelland, Rumelhart, & Hinton, 1986, pp. 3-4)

The succinct rationale clearly shows what they aimed

to achieve and the strategies they intended to use. In their subsequent explanations, this is further clarified.

> In the examples we have considered, a number of different pieces of information must be kept in mind at once. Each plays a part, constraining others and being constrained by them. What kind of mechanisms seem well suited to these task demands? Intuitively, these tasks seem to require mechanisms in which each aspect of the information in the situation can act on other aspects, simultaneously influencing other aspects and being influenced by them. To articulate these intuitions, we and other have turned to a class of models we call *Parallel Distributed Processing* (PDP) models. These models assume that information processing takes place through the interactions of a large number of simple processing elements called units, each sending excitatory and inhibitory signals to other units. ⋯ One reason for the appeal of PDP models is their obvious "physiological" flavor: They seem so much more closely tied to the physiology of the brain than are other kinds of information-processing models. ⋯ We are, after all, cognitive scientists, and PDP models appeal to us for psychological and computational reasons. They hold out the hope of offering computationally sufficient and psychologically accurate mechanistic accounts of the phenomena of human cognition ⋯ (McClelland, Rumelhart, & Hinton, 1986, pp. 10-11, italic and quotation marks in original)

To implement parallel processing models in AI, specific hardware is required to run the PDP models effectively. GPUs (Graphics Processing Units) are utilized for parallel processing in artificial neural networks (Caulfield, 2009). Commonly referred to as 'graphic cards' in personal computers, GPUs were originally developed to handle images and pictures on the monitor screen (Singer, 2023). When comparing serial and parallel processing, both the CPU (Central Processing Unit) and GPU are frequently examined (cf. Caulfield, 2009; CNBC, 2023).

The CPU excels at serial processing, handling one task at a time, whereas the GPU is designed for parallel processing, capable of managing multiple tasks simultaneously. An analogy can be made: the CPU is like "one giant soldier," taking precise shots one at a time, whereas the GPU is akin to "an army of thousand soldiers," all firing at the target together (CNBC, 2023, 5:50-6:18). Similarly, the CPU can be likened to a racing motorcycle, which is very fast and agile, representing the speed of processing, but capable of handling only a small amount of information at a time. In contrast, the GPU is comparable to a dump truck: slower and less nimble, but able to carry enormous loads of information.[49] Furthermore, GPUs operate in parallel, like a fleet of dump trucks working together, whether there are 100 or 10,000 of them. In the context of artificial neural networks and deep learning, the volume of information to be processed is literally beyond our arithmetic capability (cf. Aggarwal, 2023, pp. 452-455). In the graphical model depicted in Figure 4, for instance, each circle is connected to all (or some of) the other circles in the next layer. This configuration can involve tens of thousands of circles (technically, signaling units) and hundreds of billions (or even more) of connections

---

49 'Slower' and 'less nimble' are relative terms. They do not mean 'slow' in a literal sense; in fact, the process is incredibly fast, as many ESL educators will notice when using ChatGPT.

(technically, parameters).[50]

For a more tangible example to grasp the amount of information in artificial neural networks, imagine we ask ChatGPT about a picture. ChatGPT processes the information of the picture as a collection of particles; technically, a group of tiny pixels. For a rough example, if the resolution of our monitor is 1920X1080, then the number of pixels on our monitor would be 1920 times 1080, resulting in 2,073,600 pixels.[51] Consider that this enormous amount of data is processed rapidly every time we ask a question.

Decades ago, Crick (1995) implicitly predicted the future developments in artificial neural networks based on the advancements in AI at that time. He highlighted the potentials of these networks by considering the capabilities of the human brain.

> What can we conclude about neural networks? Their basic design is more brainlike than the architecture of a standard computer. Nevertheless, their units are not as complex as real neurons, and the architecture of most networks is grossly oversimplified compared to the circuitry of the

50 Broadly speaking, for ESL professionals, 'parameters' can be understood as estimated regression coefficients that indicate a relationship between a signal unit and an output (cf. Aggarwal, 2023, p. 74).

51 The processing is far more complex than the example, all the pixels of an image or picture are processed as a vast array of numerical signals (Aggarwal, 2023, pp. 305-318; Bishop & Bishop, 2023, pp. 291-315). Similarly, words and sentences are processed through intricate numerical computations (Aggarwal, 2023, pp 442-457; Ozdemir, 2023, pp. 15-21; Wolfram, 2023, pp. 86-109). Also refer to Branch Education (2023) for a further explanation of how the enormous amount of information in online games (far beyond our imagination) is processed via the GPU.

> neocortex. At the moment, networks have to be extremely small if they are to be simulated in a reasonable time on standard computers. This will change as computers get faster, and as highly parallel (network-like) computers are produced commercially, but it is always likely to be a serious handicap. (Crick, 1995, p. 198)

Three decades since his forecast, the majority of his predictions have materialized in our daily lives. Owing to advancements in "faster" and "highly parallel computers produced commercially," ChatGPT and other generative AI variants have permeated various aspects of our lives. Alongside their widespread adoption, both fascination and concerns have emerged regarding their impact (cf. Bloomberg Originals, 2023; CBS Mornings, 2023b; Paul G. Allen School, 2024; Patel, 2023; Sana, 2024a; Shah, 2023; Standford eCorner, 2024; Sutskever, 2023; UN News, 2024; University of Oxford, 2024; University of Toronto, 2023). These issues require collective consideration by researchers and educators within the ESL community (Coltri, 2024; Heaven, 2023b; Pack & Maloney, 2023, 2024).

CHAPTER 3

Homo sapiens and Machina sapiens

Shepherds that camp in the wild, disgraces, merest bellies:
we know to tell many lies that sound like truth,
but we know to sing reality, when we will.
(Hesiod, 730-700 BC/2008, p. 3)

Upon opening to the public at the end of 2022, ChatGPT set numerous records in online history, including the number of users within a week, the growth rate of users, and the speed of growth (Bove, 2023; Dualte, 2024; Mollman, 2022). With its phenomenal popularity, debates have been ongoing regarding the epistemological and ontological issues of ChatGPT (cf. Mitchell, 2024; Russell & Norvig, 2021, pp. 984-986). Among the debates, this evokes a galactic collision between two leading figures, Chomsky (Smith, 1999) and Hinton (Vector Institute, n.d.), from two different disciplines in terms of philosophical issues of ChatGPT: whether it has *intelligence* or not.[52]

In the article of about 1,610 words, Chomsky and his colleagues (Chomsky, Roberts, & Watumull, 2023) degrade the achievement of ChatGPT, viewing it as "something like the banality of evil: plagiarism and apathy and obviation." Seemingly opposed to the intelligence of ChatGPT by means of *thought* and *language*, their argument disguisedly disavows ChatGPT itself, as read in the concluding remark, "Given the amorality, faux science and linguistic incompetence of these systems, we can only laugh or cry at their popularity." And Hinton (University of Oxford, 2024) directly refutes them, calmly stating that

> What about language? ⋯ So, obviously many linguists are very skeptical. Chomsky managed to convince his followers that language wasn't learned. Looking back on it, that's just a completely crazy thing to say. If you can convince people to say something is obviously false, then you've got

52 For a discussion of intelligence from a critical perspective, refer to Gould (1996) and Gottfredson (1997).

> them in your cult. I think Chomsky did amazing things, but his time is over. ⋯ a big neural network with no innate knowledge could actually learn both the syntax and the semantics of language just by looking at data ⋯ (5:45-6:35)[53]

The debate over whether ChatGPT possesses *intelligence*, one indicator of which is its understanding of human language, does not seem to be solely attributed to ChatGPT's recent popularity.[54] In fact, about 30 years ago, Crick (1995) adeptly explained the differences in processing human language between human brain and artificial neural networks, and insightfully predicted the possibility of a machine possessing human-like language ability (or perhaps intelligence) in the near future.

> As linguists have emphasized, the operations of speech (such as the rules of syntax) are at the moment better handled by programs written according to A.I. theory. At bottom this is because networks are best at highly parallel processing, whereas these linguistic tasks demand a degree of serial processing. The brain has attentional systems, having a somewhat serial nature, that operate on the underlying parallel processing. So far, neural networks have not reached the degree of complexity that demands such serial processes, although this is bound to come. (Crick, 1995, pp. 196-197)

53 In his extensive discussion of consciousness and computation, Koch (2019, p. 93) maintains, "Language is the gold standard of inferring consciousness in others." For Hinton's other cogent reasons for why he thinks that ChatGPT understands in a case of French translation, see CBS Mornings (2023a, 33:10-34:58).

54 LeCun (CBS Mornings, 2023b, 0:46-1:37) began to pursue a career as an AI scientist after being intrigued by the 1970s debate between Chomsky and Piaget on whether language is learned or innate.

As anticipated, the performance of ChatGPT appears to substantiate the prediction that "[artificial] neural networks have almost reached the degree of complexity," incorporating "attentional systems with a somewhat serial nature" within a parallel processing framework. Coupled with Crick's commendable foresight in predicting future advancements, two other points in the statement are significant in relation to ChatGPT: (1) "the attentional systems" and (2) "a somewhat serial nature operating on the underlying parallel processing."

The notion of 'attention' is a well-known construct among ESL professionals. Not only has it been extensively studied in psychology (Bernstein et al., 2006, pp. 182-187), but it is also closely related to a key principle that underpins learners' success in second language acquisition, namely the 'noticing' in the Noticing Hypothesis (Schmidt, 1990). Schmidt (1990) posits that the noticing of input by L2 learners is a necessary condition for successful target language acquisition. Since his proposition, L2 researchers and educators have sought ways to facilitate learners' noticing, suggesting instructional approaches such as 'enhancing input' at lexical, syntactic, and semantic levels (Chapelle, 2003, pp. 35-68; Han, Park, & Combs, 2008; Sharwood Smith, 1993). These points are extensively described in the L2 literature.

> ··· **attention** – the psychological state of focusing on certain stimuli to the exclusion of others – can occur under both [intentional and incidental learning] conditions. One can attend, for example, to the meaning of someone's utterance either explicitly (in full awareness of the process of attending) or implicitly (without awareness). ··· [In his] **noticing hypothesis**, [Schmidt (1990)] postulates a central role for focal attention, stemming from awareness, in order

> for a learner to notice language input. (Brown, 2006, p. 292, bold in original)
>
> Noticing is of considerable theoretical importance because it accounts for which features in the input are attended to and so become intake (information stored in temporary memory which may or may not be subsequently accommodated in the interlanguage system). (Ellis, 1994, p. 361, italic in original)
>
> ⋯ the 'noticing hypothesis', suggesting that nothing is learned unless it has been noticed. Noticing does not itself result in acquisition, but it is the essential starting point. (Lightbown & Spada, 2006, p. 44)
>
> Noticing works as follows. Once a student becomes aware of a particular grammar point or language feature in input – whether through formal instruction, some type of focus-on-form activity, or repeated exposure to communicative use of the structure – he or she often continues to notice the structure in subsequent input, ⋯ Repeated noticing and continued awareness of the language feature is important because it appears to raise the student's consciousness of the structure and to facilitate restructuring of the learner's unconscious system of linguistic knowledge. Thus, when a student pays attention when receiving a grammar lesson and doing practice exercises, he or she becomes aware of the grammar feature. (Fotos, 2001, p. 272)

A key point of 'noticing' across these descriptions is encapsulated by the phrase 'pay attention.' When an L2 learner receives a large amount of input, such as written texts, radio broadcasts, television shows, or grammar lessons, it is imperative that the learner attends to specific linguistic features rather than the entirety of the input (Ellis, 1993; Park, 2011; Pica, 2005).

To process natural language (i.e., human language) effectively and efficiently, or to achieve human-like fluency and proficiency, ChatGPT emulates the attentional systems of the human brain, incorporating several analogous features (Wolfram, 2023, pp. 68-77; Ozdemir, 2023, p. 15). Conceptually, there is considerable overlap between the attentional systems in ChatGPT and the principle of 'paying attention' as emphasized in the L2 literature. Specifically, in the attentional systems in ChatGPT, 'attention' is like the selective focus described in the L2 literature. When ChatGPT is processing information, it decides which parts of the data to 'pay attention to' more than others, even if those parts are far apart (Wolfram, 2023, pp. 68-77). This helps ChatGPT's neural network make better sense of the data, by focusing on the most relevant pieces of information (Bishop & Bishop, 2023, pp. 357-360; Prince, 2023, pp. 377-408).

In the AI community, 'attention mechanisms' refer to the attentional systems, which are integral to a 'transformer.' In ChatGPT, the 'T' denotes 'transformer,' as it does in BERT.[55] Transformers are a type of artificial neural network that uses the attention mechanisms to process data (cf. Bengio, LeCun, & Hinton, 2021; Bishop & Bishop, 2023, pp. 357-360; Prince, 2023, pp. 377-408; Vaswani et al.,2017).[56] Instead of looking at

---

55 In OpenAI's ChatGPT, GPT denotes Generative Pre-trained Transformer; in Google's BERT, Bidirectional Encoder Representations from Transformers (cf. Aggarwal, 2023, p. 451).

56 A transformer, equipped with the attention mechanism and significantly improved performance, was introduced in a pivotal study by a team of AI researchers in 2017. The paper's title directly and clearly states what they aim to do: "Attention is all you need" (Vaswani et al., 2017). Long before this momentous study, efforts at consilience from various disciplines had been made, as evidenced in the preface to the 4th International

data step-by-step in order (like reading a book word by word), transformers look at all the data at once and decide, using 'attention,' which parts are important. This allows them to understand the context of the data much better and faster. The significance of 'transformers' in the history of AI is that they are "one of the most important developments in deep learning" (Bishop & Bishop, 2023, p. 357) and have "fundamentally changed the landscape of natural language processing by gradually replacing [previously developed] neural networks across the board" (Aggarwal, 2023, p. 451).[57]

By analogy, the relationship between the 'attention mechanism' and 'transformers' can be illustrated as follows. Imagine the attention mechanism as an ESL researcher who is

---

Workshop on attention in cognitive systems, WAPCV (International Workshop on Attention and Performance in Computer Vision) 2007: "Attention has been representing a core scientific topic in the design of AI-enabled systems within the last decades. Today, in the ongoing debate, design, and computational modeling of artificial cognitive systems, attention has gained a central position as a focus of research. ⋯ Attention must operate at interfaces between bottom-up driven world interpretation and top-down driven information selection, thus acting at the core of artificial cognitive systems" (Paletta & Rome, 2022, pp. 2-3). As Pinker (2009/1997, p. 12) noted, "An intelligent being cannot treat every object it sees as a unique entity unlike anything else in the universe. It has to put objects in categories so that it may apply its hard-won knowledge about similar objects encountered in the past, to the object at hand."

57 The original quote is "Transformers have fundamentally changed the landscape of natural language processing by gradually replacing recurrent neural networks across the board" (Aggarwal, 2023, p. 451). "[Recurrent Neural Networks] RNNs were first introduced in the 1980s, but have regained popularity recently due to several intellectual and hardware breakthroughs that have made them tractable to train" (Buduma, Buduma, & Papa, 2022, p. 321). And "At the heart of RNNs, is their unique ability to hold onto information, much as one holds onto memories. Unlike traditional neural networks that consider input data in isolation, RNNs have loops within them that allow the information to persist. This quality is especially useful when dealing with sequences of data, be it words in a sentence or steps in a time series" (Adams, 2024, p. 82).

examining a huge stack of journal papers on a specific topic. Instead of reading every paper word-for-word, the researcher has the capability to swiftly identify and concentrate on the most pertinent sentences from any part of the stack. This selective focus enables the researcher to efficiently synthesize essential information for writing a research paper. For the transformer, think of it as an entire research institute, where a group of such researchers employs the attention technique. Each researcher operates simultaneously, viewing different parts of the journal papers, and sharing insights with one another. The collaborative environment allows for a rapid and comprehensive understanding of complex information.[58]

Similar to the overlap of 'attention' between artificial neural networks and L2 education, the 'somewhat serial nature within the framework of parallel processes,' as previously discussed, has been recognized as a significant aspect in the field of L2 education. This topic is also explored in the L2 literature when discussing L1 acquisition as detailed by Brown (2006):

> … the generative "rule-governed" model in the Chomskyan tradition was challenged. The assumption underlying this tradition is that those generative rules, or "items" in a linguistic sense, are connected **serially**, with one connection between each pair of neurons in the brain. A "messier but more fruitful picture" (Spolsky, 1989, p. 149) was provided by what has come to be know as the **Parallel distributed**

58 For a concise and readable explanation of (1) how complicated the processing of language text is and (2) how transformers operate on language text, refer to Prince (2023, pp. 377-378).

> **processing** (PDP) model, based on the notion that information is processed simultaneously at several levels of attention. As you read the words on this page, your brain is attending to letters, word juncture and meaning, syntactic relationships, textual discourse, as well as background experiences (schemata) that you bring to the text. A child's (or adult's) linguistic performance may be the consequence of many levels of simultaneous neural interconnections rather than a serial process of one rule being applied, then another, then another and so forth. (p. 31, quotation marks and bold in original)

As stated in the explanation, it is noted that ChatGPT's linguistic performance, which parallels that of the child or the adult, is primarily driven by parallel processing but is supplemented by serial-processing approaches for specific tasks.

ChatGPT is an application that has been equipped with a series of architectures[59] through successive editions, which include "GPT, GPT-2, GPT-3, GPT-3.5, GPT-3.5 Turbo, and GPT-4,"[60] and each edition "has been an improvement over the previous one (typically by increasing the scale of the training data and by making small architectural modifications)"

59 In the context of artificial neural networks, 'architecture' refers to "the overall structure of the network: how many units it should have and how these units should be connected to each other" (Goodfellow, Bengio, & Courville, 2016, p. 191). It can be likened to the blueprint or plan of a building; however, instead of floors and rooms, it involves layers and connections. In other words, it is the detailed plan of how the network is built: how many layers it has, how many neurons are in each layer, and how all these neurons are connected and communicate with each other.

60 In May 2024, OpenAI unveiled another model, GPT-4o, in which the letter 'o' stands for 'omni' (OpenAI, 2024a; 2024b). "OpenAI's new GPT-4o model has also been called an AI agent" (Heikkilä, 2024d).

(Aggarwal, 2023, p. 452). In the development of GPT editions, two points are particularly attractive: (1) the training data and (2) its scale. Just as no human can acquire a first language from nothing, no L2 learner can learn a second language without any resources (Gleitman, Newport, & Gleitman, 1984; Krashen, 1985).

For L2 learners, input refers to what they receive regarding a target language. Input is one of the most influential topics in second language acquisition (SLA) theories, and its importance is widely recognized among ESL professionals (Krashen, 1985; Pica, 2005; Swain, 1985; Truscott & Smith, 2011). In L1 acquisition, children require a large amount of input as "rich input provides the acquirer with a better sample to work with, more opportunities to hear structures he is ready to acquire" (Gleitman, Newport, & Gleitman, 1984, p. 27). For L2 learning, learners also require input. From a cognitive perspective, *comprehensible input* is considered much better for learners than pedagogically unorganized input (Crossley, Allen, & McNamara, 2012; Krashen, 1995/1982, pp. 20-30). From a sociocultural perspective, input within the learner's "*zo-ped*"[61], or zone of proximal development (Kozulin, 1986, p. *xxxv*, italic in original), is deemed more effective than input outside *zo-*

---

61 "Vygotsky argued that the progress in concept formation by a child achieved in cooperation with an adult would be a much more sensitive gauge of the child's intellectual abilities. In this connection, Vygotsky used the term *zo-ped*, "the zone of proximal development": the place at which a child's empirically rich but disorganized spontaneous concepts "meet" the systematicity and logic of adult reasoning. As a result of such a "meeting," the weaknesses of spontaneous reasoning are compensated by the strengths of scientific logic" (Kozulin, 1986, p. *xxxv*, italic and quotation marks in original).

ped (Johnson, 2004; Lantolf, 2005; Lantolf & Beckett, 2009).[62] Although the degree of input richness is not conclusively determined in L2 learning, accumulated findings suggest that more is relatively better than less when the type of input is appropriate (cf. Ellis, 1994, pp. 269-272; Ellis & Collins, 2009).

Both the input and its richness in human language learning are equally applicable to ChatGPT. The training data serve as input for ChatGPT, and both its quantity and quality are critical to ChatGPT's model training (The Alan Turing Institute, 2023). ChatGPT operates within a large language model (LLM) framework.[63] LLMs, like GPT-3 and BERT, are constructed using the transformer architecture, which incorporates the attention mechanism. This architecture enables these models to efficiently and accurately process large amounts of text data, largely due to the attention mechanism (Bishop & Bishop, 2023, pp. 357-360; Prince, 2023, pp. 377-408; Wolfram, 2023, pp. 68-77).[64]

---

62 For a discussion of the two contrasting perspectives, cognitive and sociocultural, see Lantolf (2005, pp. 336-340).

63 LLMs are "AI models that are usually (but not necessarily) derived from the Transformer architecture and are designed to *understand* and *generate* human language, code, and much more. These models are trained on vast amounts of text data, allowing them to capture the complexities and nuances of human language. LLMs can perform a wide range of language-related tasks, from simple text classification to text generation, with high accuracy, fluency, and style" (Ozdemir, 2023, p. 3, italic in original). A prototype of LLMs was introduced in 2001, as Ruder (2018) illustrated, "The first neural language model, ··· was proposed in 2001 by Bengio et al. (2001, 2003) ··· Language modeling is a form of unsupervised learning, which Yann LeCun also calls predictive learning and cites as a prerequisite to acquiring common sense."

64 As a matter of fact, the entire structure and process is tremendously complicated both physically (i.e., the gigantic scale of linguistic data) and mathematically (i.e., the huge matrix calculation with more than 3 dimensions) (cf. Prince, 2023, pp. 377-408; Wolfram,

The scale of input for ChatGPT, as the name of the model indicates, is large. Hinton (University of Oxford, 2024) shares the story of how large is what LLMs deal with in learning language:

> So, the idea that a big neural network with no innate knowledge could actually learn both the syntax and the semantics of language just by looking at data was regarded as completely crazy by statisticians and cognitive scientists. I had statisticians, explained to me, "A big model has 100 parameters;[65] the idea of learning a million parameters is just stupid." Well, we're doing a trillion now. (6:25-6:47)[66]

As illustrated, LLMs are "massive and use large training data

---

2023, pp. 68-77). Language input is transformed into numerical values (or encoded input) and then this numerical information is processed. For a better understanding of this complexity, as well as introductory AI materials in the AI literature, it is helpful to have a basic knowledge of two terms from physics and mathematics: *scalar* and *vector*. For further explanation of these terms, see Appendix.

65 Suppose a statistical model familiar to many ESL professionals: a multiple regression model. In the regression model, there are 100 independent variables (i.e., the number of X variables is 100). Indeed, this is a big model. Some statistical textbooks for social and behavioral scientists suggest a minimum sample size of about 20 participants per X variable in the regression model (e.g., Stevens, 2002). In practice, however, the rule of thumb for the sample size is 'the more, the better' (cf. Hayes, 2005; Jaeger, 1984; Pedhazur, 1997). Considering a minimum sample size for a regression model with 100 independent variables, the model would require a sample of at least 2,000 participants.

66 One trillion, represented as 1,000,000,000,000, consists of 12 zeros and epitomizes a quantity far beyond the scope of human comprehension. Christ was born approximately 2,024 years ago; the total number of days since his birth is 738,760. Buddha is believed to have been born around 623 BC; the total number of days since that epoch is 966,155. Modern *Homo sapiens* are estimated to have first appeared approximately 160,000 years ago; the total number of days since their appearance is 584 million. Earth, our planetary home, is estimated to be about 4.5 billion years old; the total number of days since its formation is approximately 1.6 trillion.

sets with hundreds of billions of parameters" and "the effect of training data and model size has been truly remarkable in terms of learning the ability to perform a wide variety of language processing" (Aggarwal, 2023, p. 451). Specifically, the scale of training data for ChatGPT is known to consist of 300 billion tokens, and its LLM utilizes 175 billion parameters (cf. Prince, 2023, p. 407; Wolfram, 2023, p. 21). In a general sense, a 'token' is equivalent to a word "even though GPT-3 (BERT) token is not really a word from the semantic perspective" (Aggarwal, 2023, p. 453).[67] Prince (2023, p. 407) provides a further details: "In GPT3, the sequence lengths are 2048 tokens long, and the total batch size is 3.2 million tokens.[68] There are 96 transformers (some of which implement a sparse version of attention), each processing a word embedding of size 12288."

The phrase, 'a word embedding,' is a technical term, and understanding the meaning of 'embedding' more clearly requires mathematical explanation.[69] Yet, Wolfram (2023) helps to conceptually grasp the general meaning of 'a word embedding':

> [artificial] Neural nets – at least as they're currently set up – are fundamentally based on numbers. So if we're going to use them to work on something like text we'll need a way to represent out text with numbers. And certainly we

67 To explore the relationship between the number of English words and the number of tokens in GPT, refer to the OpenAI tokenizer at https://platform.openai.com/tokenizer

68 With the entire training data, ChatGPT is trained through an iterative process to optimize its predictions. "At each iteration, the algorithm chooses a random subset of the training data and compute [the optimization] from these examples alone. This subset is known as a *minibatch* or *batch* for short" (Prince, 2023, p. 152, italic in original).

69 For further explanation of 'embedding,' see Appendix.

> could start (essentially as ChatGPT does) by just assigning a number to every word in the dictionary. But there's an important idea ⋯ And it's the idea of "embeddings". One can think of an embedding as a way to try to represent the "essence" of something by an array of numbers – with the property that "nearby things" are represented by nearby numbers. And so, ⋯, we can think of a word embedding as trying to lay out words in a kind of "meaning space" in which words that are somehow "nearby in meaning" appear nearby in the embedding. (p. 60, quotation marks in original)

At the risk of oversimplifying, a word embedding can be understood as a vocabulary village where words "nearby in meaning" stay together. Furthermore, the notion of 'embedding' can be understood in relation to coding linguistic tokens in corpus analysis in L2 literature. As Biber and Conrad (2009) confessed,

> [p]rincipled, consistent classifying of language features can be a surprisingly difficult task. Most people learn grammar from textbooks that have easy, clear-cut examples. But natural texts, from different registers, almost always contain linguistic forms that do not fit tidily into the textbook categories.[70] (p. 59)

Wolfram's (2023) "meaning space" can be expressed

---

70 For further details about the complexity of natural texts (e.g., the same word should be considered an adjective in one sentence and a noun in another), see Biber and Conrad (2009, pp. 59-61).

differently in the description by Biber, Connor, and Upton (2007):

> Text types and genres (or register) represent complementary ways to dissect the textual space of a language. Text types and genres/registers are similar in that both can be described in linguistic and in situational/functional terms. However, the two constructs differ in their primary bases: genres/registers are defined in terms of their situational characteristics, while text types are defined linguistically.
>
> (p. 172)[71]

Similar to the process of human language acquisition, the volume of input is paramount for ChatGPT's learning of human languages. As demonstrated in the left graph of Figure 6, there is a positive correlation, albeit non-linear, between input scale and performance outcomes: larger scales yield improved performance (cf. Ananthaswamy, 2023; Brown et al., 2020; Frank, 2023; Hoffmann et al., 2022). Additionally, a notable phenomenon related to this scalability is observed: performance gradually improves with increased scale until it reaches a critical point, at which it dramatically spikes as presented in the right graph of Figure 6. This phenomenon, known as an 'emergent ability,' which refers to "*an ability is emergent if it is not present in smaller models but is present in larger models*" (Wei et al.,

---

71 For details on how vocabulary-based discourse units are classified within the textual space, see Biber, Connor, and Upton (2007, pp. 169-173). Note that Wolfram (2023, p. 60) uses the term, "meaning space," and Biber, Connor, and Upton (2007, p. 172) use the term, "the textual space." Technically, 'a word embedding' is mathematically represented in the embedding vector space (cf. Russell & Norvig, 2021, pp. 856-860).

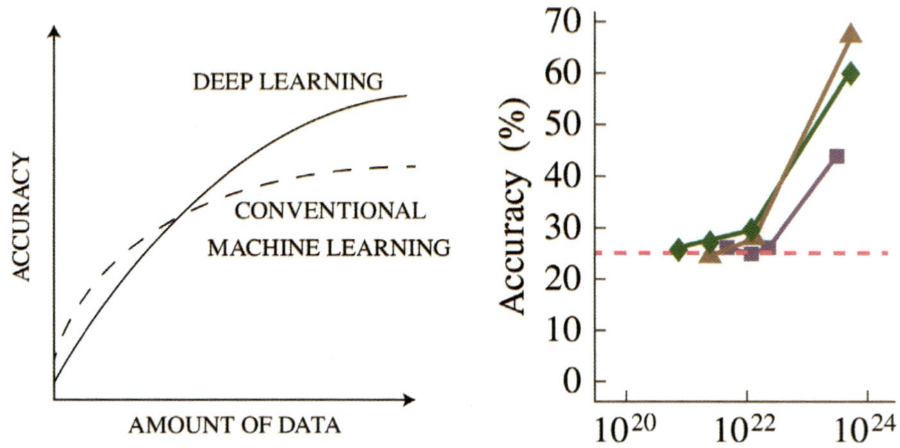

Figure 6. A relationship between the scale of data and accuracy in deep learning (left), and the emergent abilities in LLMs (right): The left graph is a replica from Aggarwal (2023, p. 3), and the right graph replicates "Figure 2G" from Wei et al. (2022, p. 4), concerning massive multi-task language understanding. In the right graph, the purple line indicates GPT-3, and the horizontal axis indicates the data scale.

2022, p. 2, italic in original). The emergent ability observed in LLMs remains enigmatic in terms of its underlying mechanisms and is currently being extensively studied by AI researchers (Brown et al., 2020; Frank, 2023; Hoffmann et al., 2022; Kaplan et al., 2020; Ornes, 2024; Wei et al., 2022).

The point regarding the relationship between the scale of training data in LLMs and their performance can be clearly summarized by Wolfram's (2023) comment:

> How were all those 175 billion weights[72] in its neural net determined? Basically they're the result of very large-scale training, based on a huge corpus of text – on the web, in books, etc. – written by humans. As we've said, even given all that training data, it's certainly not obvious that a neural net would be able to successfully produce "human-like" text. And, once again, there seem to be detailed pieces of engineering needed to make that happen. But the big surprise – and discovery – of ChatGPT is that it's possible at all. And that – in effect – a neural net with "just" 175 billion weights can make a "reasonable model" of text humans write. (p. 79, quotation marks in original)

ChatGPT demonstrates remarkable performance, although the definitive existence of its intelligence remains unresolved. Despite this, researchers stay on *the stream of artificial consciousness* in their quest for empirical evidence. Mitchell and her colleagues (2023) recently conducted an experimental study to investigate whether ChatGPT possesses intelligence

72 The term 'weights' is equivalent to 'parameters' or 'estimated coefficients.' In many AI materials, 'weights' or 'parameters' are generally preferred over 'coefficients.'

by comparing its capacity for abstract reasoning with that of humans, concluding that GPT-4 does not exhibit "robust abstraction abilities at human-like levels" (p. 1). Alongside, Roivainen (2023) evaluated AI's Intelligence Quotient; and Choi (2022, 2023), on the other hand, probes the potential of AI to present common sense comparable to human capabilities. Furthermore, research initiatives proceed in the development of Artificial General Intelligence (AGI) (Mitchell, 2024; Morris et al., 2024; Patel, 2023; Sutskever, 2023).[73] In addition, advancements in generative AI technology have spurred the creation of models with diverse parameter scales and more compact designs (Moniz, et al., 2024), as well as developments in more human-like interactive AIs, such as ChatGPT-4o (Heikkilä, 2024d; OpenAI, 2024a, 2024b), and humanoid robots equipped with both brain and brawn (Boston Dynamics, 2024; CNBC, 2024a).

In light of the advancement and enhanced performance of generative AI technologies thus far, the relevance of questioning whether ChatGPT is intelligent appears substantially moot (cf. Heaven, 2024c). While this issue may hold importance for certain researchers who either support or oppose the notion of 'being intelligent,' it may not resonate similarly among the broader public, including students, educators, administrators, and business professionals (cf. Heaven, 2023a; Omar et al., 2024; Overgoor et al., 2019; Pack & Maloney, 2023; Shah,

73 "The term "AGI" was coined in the early 2000s to recapture the original lofty aspirations of AI pioneers, seeking a renewed focus on "attempts to study and reproduce intelligence as a whole in a domain independent way" (Mitchell, 2024, quotation marks in original).

2023). Instead, users of ChatGPT predominantly appreciate its ability to replicate human-like speaking and writing, focusing less on whether it is actually intelligent (OpenAI, 2024c). The environment in which ordinary people work and live is becoming a milieu where the significance of validating such a 'being' issue is diminishing (Li, 2024; Omar et al., 2024; Patel, 2023; Shah, 2023; Standford eCorner, 2024; Sutskever, 2023; The Alan Turing Institute, 2023; University of Oxford, 2024; Wolfram, 2023). Currently, ChatGPT and other generative AI systems represent an artificial craft within an emerging phenomenon, one that remains unable to definitively prove its instantiated intelligence (Blackford & Broderick, 2014; Bostrom, 2014; Kurzweil, 2005; Simon, 2019).[74]

74 To a large extent, the present debates concerning the presence of intelligence in ChatGPT hark back to historical debates among mathematicians regarding the concept of imaginary numbers (namely the square roots of negative numbers) approximately 300 years ago. In adaptation of Leibniz's articulation, ChatGPT's intelligence can be describe as "an elegant and marvelous trick found in the miracle of [advances in digital technologies]: a monster of the ideal world, almost an amphibian located somewhere between Being and non-Being" (requoted and adapted from Hofstadter & Sander, 2013, p. 442). Hofstadter and Sander (2013) provide a depiction of what transpired at the time: "As mathematicians gradually got used to the fact that these mysterious expressions acted in many ways just as ordinary numbers do, ⋯ the objecting voices slowly faded away ⋯ Gottfried Wilhelm von Leibniz, co-inventor with Isaac Newton of the infinitesimal calculus, described in 1702, the numbers that René Descartes had dubbed "imaginary": "an elegant and marvelous trick found in the miracle of Analysis: a monster of the ideal world, almost an amphibian located somewhere between Being and non-Being." And even Leonhard Euler, the Swiss genius who deserves enormous credit for putting the theory of complex numbers on a solid footing, declared, on the subject of the square roots of negative numbers, that they are "not nothing, nor less than nothing, which makes them imaginary, indeed impossible" (p. 442, quotation marks in original).

Chapter 4

Il buono, Il brutoo, Il cattivo[75]

K.A.R.R.: KITT, I am warning you. Change course at once!
K.I.T.T.: I am not in control, KARR.
K.A.R.R.: Then tell the humans to turn away. This is folly, KITT.

...

K.I.T.T.: Michael, what are you doing?

...

K.A.R.R.: Your lives mean nothing to me!
K.I.T.T.: Michael, please. Pardon the expression, but he does have a few screws loose. Turn. KARR doesn't have my programming to protect human life.

...

The Rev: Yeah. You can't count on nobody 'cept me and Tony.
K.A.R.R.: Interesting. I will enter that information in my databanks. I am indebted to both of you. You have reactivated me. How may I serve you?
Tony: *[burps]* Serve us? What do you mean, serve us?
K.A.R.R.: I have checked my data on basic human desires. Therefore, I understand your needs.

(Larson et al., 1982)[76]

75 The title originates from Italian one (Leone, 1966); in English, *The Good, The Bad and The Ugly*.

76 The transcript is from https://www.imdb.com/title/tt0620882/characters/nm0191520

ChatGPT's exceptional performance has sparked public fascination and excitement, reminiscent of the response to the unveiling of the Perceptron approximately 70 years ago. However, the excitement has recently faltered. This shift is not attributed to deficiencies in ChatGPT's performance; rather, it is because its capabilities are so preeminent that they are poised to soon surpass human capacities, both physical and mental (Alexander, 2024; Else, 2023; Heaven, 2023a; Pack & Maloney, 2023). A symbolic example of this dithering over the advancement of generative AI is Hinton's resignation from the advisory boards of major AI tech companies. His proactive effort to publicly highlight the potential dangers associated with AI's rapid advancements cautions that its exceptional capabilities necessitate more measured approaches to development (cf. Amanpour and Company, 2023; Heaven, 2023b, 2024d; MIT Technology Review, 2023; University of Oxford, 2024; University of Toronto, 2023). The heightened awareness of the risks has spread widely among societal leaders, researchers, and the public.

In May 2024, global leaders convened at the United Nations' (UN's) AI for Good Global Summit to deliberate on the dual aspects of "the hope and fear of AI development" (UN News, 2024). The summit primarily assessed the alignment of recent AI advancements with the UN's Sustainable Development Goals (SDGs).[77] However, the explicit mention of "fear" highlights an escalating concern about both the rapid pace of AI advancements and their significant achievements. Heikkilä

77 For details about the SDGs, see https://sdgs.un.org

(2024b) provides an analysis of the post-conference sentiments, emphasizing a predominant inclination towards "fear" rather than "hope":

> But honestly, I didn't leave the conference feeling confident AI was going to play a meaningful role in advancing any of the UN goals. In fact, the most interesting speeches were about how AI is doing the opposite. ··· how we must not let AI accelerate environmental destruction. ··· there are still deeply ingrained gender biases in tech, ··· So while the conference itself was about using AI for "good," I would have liked to see more talk about how increased transparency, accountability, and inclusion could make AI *itself* good from development to deployment. We now know that generating one image with generative AI uses as much energy as charging a smartphone.[78] (quotation marks and italic in original)

Heikkilä (2024b) summarized the essence of pressing AI issues in three key words: transparency, accountability, and inclusion (cf. Coeckelbergh, 2020, pp. 145-163; Coltri, 2024;

---

78 For further discussion of generative AI and its vast energy consumption, see Chen (2024), CNBC (2024b), and Heikkilä (2022a). In addition, Wooldridge (The Alan Turing Institute, 2023, 27:12-28:03) provided a brief illustration and a meaningful implication regarding the scale of energy consumption by ChatGPT and who can afford it: "In order to be able to train the neural networks with all of [the vast] training data ··· you require extremely expensive AI supercomputers running for months. And, by extremely expensive AI supercomputers, these are tens of millions of dollars for these supercomputers and they're running for months. Just the basic electricity cost runs into millions of dollars. That raises all sorts of issues about CO_2 emissions and the like that. ··· The point is, these are extremely expensive things. One of the implications of that, by the way, no UK or US has the capability to build one of these models from scratch. It's only big tech companies at the moment that are capable of building models on the scale of GPT3 or ChatGPT."

Diakopoulos, 2020; Dignum, 2020; Gabriel & Ghazavi, 2023; Kroll, 2020; Liao & Vaughan, 2023; Mittelstadt, 2023; Novelli, Taddeo, & Floridi, 2023; Russell & Norvig, 2021, pp.986-1005). Transparency means that the processes and decisions made by an AI system are clear and understandable to its users and stakeholders (Diakopoulos, 2020; Mittelstadt, 2023). This involves explaining how the AI works, what data it uses, and how it reaches its decisions. Accountability refers to ensuring that there are systems at the societal level in place to hold the developers and users of AI systems responsible for how their technology impacts people and society (Dignum, 2020; Kroll, 2020; Novelli, Taddeo, & Floridi, 2023). It includes taking responsibility for mistakes or harm caused by the outcomes of AI systems. Inclusion means designing and deploying AI systems in ways that they consider and respect the diverse needs, abilities, and perspectives of all community members, especially those who are typically marginalized or underrepresented (Cachat-Rosset & Klarsfeld, 2023; Coeckelbergh, 2020, pp. 145-163; Rizk, 2020).

The three terms Heikkilä (2024b) employs are not merely rhetorical enticements; they signify substantial concerns among both AI researchers and the general public. Illustrative of these concerns are several documented examples: AI-controlled military aircraft have reportedly attacked human operators (Davis & Squire, 2023; Kleinman, 2023), and AI has been used anonymously to create fake news and false identities for illegal and unethical purposes (Heikkilä, 2024a, 2024c; Mahari & Pataranutaporn, 2024). Furthermore, the academic community has observed AI being employed in deceptive practices designed to mislead scientists (Heikkilä, 2022b; Else, 2023), and there are persistent worries about AI's disruptive effects on the arts (Williams, 2024). These instances accentuate the broad and critical challenges that AI presents across various domains (cf. Bengio, 2023; Berkman Klein Center, 2019; Center for AI Safety, n.d.; Coltri, 2024; Eye on AI, 2023; Hendrycks, Mazeika, & Woodside, 2023; Park et al., 2024; Russell, 2019).

What strategies might we employ to address these concerns? To effectively tackle them, it may be essential to shift our focus back to humans rather than relying on machines (Bennett, 2023; Dennett, 1981/1978, pp. 190-229; Hutson, 2024; Larson, 2022; Simon, 2019/1969, pp. 51-138; Wolfram, 2023).[79] This approach suggests that humans themselves hold the key to resolving these challenges, not the AI systems. Exploring two separate but interrelated descriptions will give us food for thought on how to resolve the challenges. For instance, in comparing the human brain with those of other animals, Eagleman (2015) details the distinctive features and capabilities that set it apart:

> The human brain comes into the world with some amount of genetic hardwiring (for example, for breathing, crying, suckling, caring about faces, and having the ability to learn the details of their native language). But compared to the rest of the animal kingdom, human brains are unusually incomplete at birth. The detailed wiring diagram of the human brain is not preprogrammed; instead, genes give very general directions for the blueprints of neural networks, and world experience fine-tunes the rest of the wiring, allowing it to adapt to the local details. (p. 8)

---

79 In a broadcast interview, a host asked, "Yesterday, Nick Frost, who used to work with you, told us that you are not really that interested in creating AI. Your core interest is just in understanding how the brain works?" Hinton replied, "Yes, I'd really like to understand how the brain works" (CBS Mornings, 2023a, 3:38-3:49).

The unique capability of the human brain has an intriguing connection to the recent discoveries presented in Frank (2023), which can be comprehensively interpreted across both contexts.

> For many observers, the most interesting feature of LLMs is their ability to reason flexibly about new tasks based on a verbal query, ··· This behavior, sometimes termed 'few shot' or 'in-context learning'[80], appears to emerge only at very large scales of training data. Yet another type of intelligence performs in-context learning with far less data than even the smallest of LLMs: human. From an early age, children can reason flexibly about novel tasks, and by middle childhood they can quickly master new games, devices, and environments. What can we learn about human and machine intelligence by comparing their data efficiency?
>
> (Frank, 2023, p. 990)

The two separate but interrelated descriptions reveal

---

80 In the context of LLMs, 'fine-tuning,' 'few-shot learning,' and 'in-context learning' are technical terms (cf. Brown et al., 2020; Goodfellow, Bengio, & Courville, 2016, p. 314; Ozdemir, 2023, pp. 77-94; Prince, 2023, pp. 407-408). 'Fine-tuning' entails actual training during which the model's parameters (weights) are updated. After an LLM has been pre-trained on a large dataset to learn a broad understanding of language, fine-tuning further adjusts these learned parameters to tailor the model for more specific tasks or datasets. 'Few-shot learning' involves presenting the model with a few examples of a task during the inference phase to guide its predictions. The LLM uses these examples to better understand the task it needs to perform. Similarly, 'in-context learning' involves the model with contextual examples directly within the prompt. The model uses these examples to infer the pattern or the task required and generates a response based on the context provided. The model uses the context to make predictions without modifying its underlying parameters. The distinctive point is that both few-shot and in-context learning are not 'post-training learning' methods in the sense that the model does not continue to learn or update its parameters after initial training.

both overlaps and distinctions between humans and LLMs. Upon initial observation, the human brain and LLMs appear distinctly juxtaposed, with a clear symmetrical contrast in presentation. However, beneath the superficial distinction lies a fundamental alignment in functional capabilities. Notably, children demonstrate the capacity to adapt to new tasks using significantly less data (indicative of circumscribed schematic knowledge) from an early age. This form of adaptability is paralleled in ChatGPT, which, despite requiring extensive training on large datasets, displays similar flexible responses. At first glance, ChatGPT may seem considerably less capable than children; yet, when their learning processes are examined more closely, the similarities become apparent. Additionally, the potential for ChatGPT to achieve capacities comparable to those of children is more promising than restrictive.

As Frank (2023) demonstrates, there is a disparity in the scale of language input between humans and ChatGPT (GPT-3). By the age of 10, children have learned an average of about 107.5 words of language input, which increases to an average of about 108 words by the age of 20. In stark contrast, GPT-3 begins its training with approximately 1012 words of language input, maintaining the scale throughout. Remarkably, the language input scale for humans at the age of 20 is about 10,000 times smaller than that of GPT-3. Nevertheless, despite the vast quantitative advantage, GPT-3 significantly lags behind humans in its capacity to grasp conceptual knowledge and engage in reasoning (cf. Mitchell, Palmarini, & Moskvichev, 2023).

Upon its release to the public in 2022, ChatGPT underwent numerous tests by people around the world to assess whether it truly understood human language and could communicate like humans (Duarte, 2024; Johnson, 2023; Mollman, 2022). During these tests, many testers pointed out its nonsensical and often humorous responses, commonly referred to as *hallucinations*, which describe instances where ChatGPT produces statements that are untrue or illogical (Choi, 2023; Heaven, 2024a, 2024b; Takahashi, 2023). About two years after its debut, the issue of hallucinations has become significantly less pronounced (Heaven, 2024b). Those who remain concerned, particularly non-AI professionals, may continue to contend that the occurrence of hallucinations is unavoidable in ChatGPT (or in LLMs), potentially attributable to its nature as a machine, namely its lack of human-like intelligence, or to its reliance on a statistical model that computes based on probabilities. Although these arguments may possess some validity, they are not conclusively definitive at present, as the performances of upgraded LLMs are becoming more accurate and precise (cf. OpenAI, 2024c).

A reconsideration of hallucinations from an alternative viewpoint may yield a varied understanding. The issue of hallucinations, as perceived by the public, is likely to be associated with two contradictory public expectations: (1) computers should unfailingly deliver accurate responses; (2) their intelligence is not yet sufficient to reach human levels. Given that LLMs are engineered to replicate human neural networks, their outputs can mirror human-like inconsistencies. This prompts the question: Are humans themselves always truthful, or are they devoid of fabrication? As Kish (1978, p. 2) states, "To err is human, to forgive divine – but to include errors in your design is statistical." Could it then be said, "To err is AI, to accept human – but to include errors in your architecture is also statistical?"[81]

In the discussion of developing a machine that feels 'human-like pain,' Dennette (1981/1978, p. 191) emphasizes the importance of 'a good theory' through the example of "a good computer simulation of a hurricane."

> Consider, for instance, a good computer simulation of a hurricane, as might be devised by meteorologists. One would not expect to get wet or wind-blown in its presence. That ludicrous expectation would be akin to a use-mention error, like cowering before the word "lion". A good computer simulation of a hurricane is a program, which, when you feed in *descriptions* of new meteorological conditions, gives you back *descriptions* of subsequent hurricane behavior. ⋯ Such a program is tantamount to an immense conjunction of complicated conditions: ⋯ Obviously the only way to populate that conjunction reliably is by deriving the particular conditionals from general covering laws, all properly meshed and coordinated. So in order to write a good simulation program, one must have a *theory* of hurricane behavior, and it must be a good theory. (Dennette, 1981/1978, p. 191, quotation marks and italic in original)

Considering the emphasis he places and the fact that

81 Deep learning models, in their simplest form, can be thought of as complex extensions of basic predictive modeling techniques such as multiple regression. Aggarwal (2023) succinctly explains its baseline: "One way of viewing deep learning models is as a network connecting simpler computational units like the perceptron. Two examples of such simpler models are *linear regression* and *logistic regression*" (p. 74, italic in original). In illustrating the features of multiple regression for social and behavioral scientists, Cohen (1968, p. 426) described multiple regression as "a general data-analysis system."

ChatGPT is modeled after human neural networks, it becomes apparent that a robust theoretical framework is necessary – a theory of human cognition, particularly a good theory of the brain. This necessity becomes evident from our current level of self-understanding.

> When humanity wanted to understand flight, we garnered our first inspiration from birds; when George de Mestral invented Velcro, he got the idea from burdock fruits; when Benjamin Franklin sought to explore electricity, his first sparks of understanding came from lightning. Nature has, throughout the history of human innovation, long been a wondrous guide. Nature also offers us clues as to how intelligence works – the clearest locus of which is, of course, the human brain. ⋯ the brain has proven to be more unwieldy and harder to decipher than either wings or lightning. Scientists have been investigating how the brain works for millennia, and while we have made progress, we do not yet have satisfying answers. The problem is complexity. (Bennett, 2023, pp. 3-4)

As Bennett (2023) notes, despite significant advancements, our understanding of the human brain remains unfulfilled (Barrett, 2020; Gould, 1996; Koch, 2019; Sapolsky, 2017).[82]

---

82 "The brain of the great mathematician K. F. Gauss (right) proved to be something of an embarrassment since, at 1,492 grams, it was only slightly larger than average. But other criteria came to the rescue. Here, E. A. Spitzka demonstrates that Gauss's brain is much more richly convoluted than that of a Papuan (left)" (Gould, 1996/1981, p. 125). Bennett (2023, p. 254) explained the relationship between brain size and its newly added functions: "most evidence suggests that despite the dramatic expansion in size, the brain of our primate ancestor, and of primates today, was largely the same as that of the early mammals. A bigger hindbrain, a bigger basal ganglia, a bigger neocortex, but still all the same regions

Given the complexity of the human brain, which contains about 86 billion neurons and approximately 1000 trillion neural connections, fully understanding it poses substantial challenges (Barrett, 2020; Koch, 2019; Larson, 2022; Sapolsky, 2017). In contrast, while ChatGPT, with its 175 billion parameters, exhibits remarkable performance (Wolfram, 2023), it does not fully meet the expectations of many users due to its incomplete performance. A problem with this discrepancy, however, is that even though ChatGPT has a relatively simple architecture compared to the human brain, its performance is exceptionally good; yet, the reasons for this effectiveness remain unclear. This issue is more directly addressed in the subsequent description.

> But with conventional software, someone with inside knowledge can usually deduce what's going on, Bau [a computer scientist] says. If a website's ranking drops in a Google search, for example, someone at Google – where Bau worked for a dozen years – will have a good idea why. "Here's what really terrifies me" about the current breed of artificial intelligence (AI), he says: "there is no such understanding", even among the people building it. … These patterns can be inscrutable to humans. The most advanced machine-learning systems use neural networks: software inspired by the architecture of the brain. They simulate layers of neurons, which transform information as it passes from layer to layer. As in human brains, these networks strengthen and weaken neural connections as they learn, but it's hard to see why certain connections are

---

connected in all the same fundamental ways. These early primates indeed dedicated disproportionately more neocortex to certain functions, such as vision and touch, but still, the functions and connectivity were largely the same."

> affected. As a result, researchers often talk about AI as 'black boxes', the inner workings of which are mystery. (Hutson, 2024, pp. 986-987, quotation marks in original)

What Hutson (2024) states is that the processes occurring within the hidden layers of deep learning models are veiled, comparable to 'black boxes.'[83] This is further elucidated through a series of statements by Wolfram (2023) analyzing the internals of ChatGPT.

> There's nothing particularly "theoretically derived" about this neural net; it's just something that – back in 1998 – was constructed as a piece of engineering, and found to work. (Of course, that's not much different from how we might describe our brains as having been produced through the process of biological evolution.) (p. 27, quotation marks and parentheses in original)
>
> But at least as of now we don't have a way to "give a narrative description" of what the network is doing. ⋯ and there's no general way to find what it does except by explicitly tracing each step. Or maybe it's just that we haven't "figured out the science", and identified the "natural laws" that allow us to summarize what's going on. (p. 37, quotation marks in original)
>
> What determines this structure? Ultimately it's presumably some "neural net encoding" of features of human language. But as of now, what those features might be is

83 The notion of a 'black box' is familiar to many ESL professionals, as it has been used to explain human linguistic abilities in the fields of L1 and L2 acquisition (cf. Chomsky, 1968; Cook, 1983; White, 2003).

> quite unknown. In effect, we're "opening up the brain of ChatGPT" (or at least GPT-2) and discovering, yes, it's complicated in there, and we don't understand it – even through in the end it's producing recognizable human language. (p. 74, quotation marks in original)

Implying the utmost importance of "a good theory" (Dennett, 1981/1978, p. 191) and bolstered by the three corroborative statements (Bennett, 2023; Hutson, 2024; Wolfram, 2023), Simon (2019/1969) provides an illustrative example that comprehensively summarizes the series of preceding statements.

> We watch an ant make his laborious way across a wind- and wave-molded beach. He moves ahead, angles to the right to ease his climb up a steep dunelet, detours around a pebble, stops for a moment to exchange information with a compatriot. Thus he makes his weaving, halting way back to his home. ⋯ I sketch the path on a piece of paper. It is a sequence of irregular, angular segments – not quite a random walk, for it has an underlying sense of direction, of aiming toward a goal. I show the unlabeled sketch to a friend. Whose path is it? An expert skier, perhaps, slaloming down a steep and somewhat rocky slope. ⋯ Whoever made the path, and in whatever space, why is it not straight; why does it not aim directly from its starting point to its goal? In the case of the ant (and for that matter the others) we know the answer. He has a general sense of where home lies, but he cannot foresee all the obstacles between. He must adapt his course repeatedly to the difficulties he encounters and often detour uncrossable barriers. ⋯ Viewed as a geometric figure, the ant's path is irregular, complex, hard to describe. But its complexity is really a complexity in the surface of the beach, not a

> complexity in the ant. On that same beach another small creature with a home at the same place as the ant might well follow a very similar path. (Simon, 2019/1969, p. 51)

Simon's depiction of the ant and the beach effectively illustrates the necessary response to address the challenges arising between ChatGPT and humans. The focus should not merely dwell on generative AI but should extend to "the nature of human intelligence itself – how it works, why it works the way it does" (Bennett, 2023, p. 3). In alignment with these thoughts, Bostrom (2014, p. 42) contends that detailed knowledge about neurons, synapses, axons, and dendrites, along with their interactions, is crucially linked to the success of developing a brain emulation, which "is not yet available even for the smallest nervous systems."

In light of this, it would be appropriate to recognize that the inconsistencies and unpredictability observed in ChatGPT's performance may not be directly attributed to ChatGPT itself. Instead, these phenomena can be seen as reflections of our limited understanding of human cognitive processes, emphasizing the need for further development of our theoretical frameworks to explain human cognition. "In searching for explanations, [we] inevitably encounter difficulties" (Lear, 1988, p. 173).[84] Furthermore, as we navigate these challenges, "[u]ncertainty, in the presence of vivid hopes and fears, is painful, but must be endured if we wish to live without the support of comforting fairy tales" (Russell,

84 The original quote, "In searching for explanations, men inevitably encounter difficulties," is from Lear (1988, p.173), who referenced Aristotle's *Metaphysics*.

1972/1945, p. xiv). Thus, the issues associated with ChatGPT should be perceived not merely as technological shortcomings but as reflections of broader limitations in our understanding of ourselves. This understanding should serve as a fundamental principle guiding AI users, including ESL professionals, in addressing these challenges. Until these issues are fundamentally resolved, ESL professionals must develop strategic approaches to engaging with generative AI and cultivate the necessary discernment for its effective use.

Part II

Chapter 5

AI and ESL Education: From *CALL 3.0* toward *CALL 4.0*?

What a piece of work is a man!
How noble in reason, how infinite in faculty,
in form and moving how express and admirable,
in action how like an angel,
in apprehension how like a god – the beauty of the world,
the paragon of animal!

(Shakespeare, 1603/1997, p. 325)

Computers (or machines) were first introduced into the field of L2 education approximately 100 years ago, though the exact timeline may vary depending on the pedagogical or technological criteria used by CALL researchers (cf. Chapelle, 2001, pp. 1-26; Otto, 2017; Pennington, 1996a; Warschauer & Healey, 1998). The quintessential roles that computers have assumed and their integration into L2 education throughout the century are concisely captured in the concluding remarks of Otto (2017), who reviewed an extensive body of CALL literature spanning from the early 1900s to the 2010s.

> While the fundamental media used in language instruction – text, audio, video, images – have remained constant over time, their technological formats and their role in language learning have changed dramatically. ⋯ Regardless of how one describes the history of CALL, it is indisputable that technology has in fact become more integrated into language learning and is well on the way to becoming a normal part of everyday practice. (p. 20)

Before the 1970s, numerous initiatives were launched and a variety of proposals were put forward concerning the use of then-current technology for L2 teaching and learning (Otto, 2017, pp. 10-12). Nevertheless, the advent of mainframe computers in the early 1970s significantly underlined their potential to enhance L2 education across a broader spectrum (Chapelle, 2001, pp. 3-4). Since then, theoretical and pedagogical approaches to utilizing computers in L2 education have evolved progressively and more systematically, in tandem with advancements in computer technology (cf. Chapelle, 2001, pp. 44-94). In addition, the proliferation of personal computers in the 1980s significantly expanded access for L2 educators (Time, 1983). During the period, an increasing number of L2 researchers turned their attention to systematically exploring previously uncharted territories within various subfields of L2 education, facilitated by the widespread adoption of personal computers (Otto, 2017, pp. 14-16). By the 1990s, the discourse concerning computer integration had progressively transformed from questioning "whether the computer *should be* used" to "how can the computer best be used" (Chapelle, 2001, p. 1, italic in original). Such fundamental change is evident in numerous CALL studies in the 1990s, in a context where a variety of software tools for L2 teachers and learners were introduced and gained widespread utilization (e.g., Chun & Plass, 1996; Johns, 1994; Pennington, 1996b). Additionally, Chapelle's (2001) use of specific acronyms in her comprehensive discussion of computer integration into L2 education distinctly illustrates the shifting emphasis on CALL throughout the decade.

CACD	Computer-assisted classroom discussion
CASLA	Computer applications in second language acquisition
CALT	Computer-assisted language testing
CASLR	Computer-assisted second language research
CAT	Computer adaptive testing
CMC	Computer-mediated communication

(Chapelle, 2001, p. xvii)

Extending from this line of thought, Egbert (2005) sought to analyze CALL systematically, with a specific emphasis on the importance of "*context*" in its conceptualization (p. 4, italic in original). Within her framework, computers in L2 pedagogy effectively address spatial constraints (such as schools, homes, classrooms, or cafés), temporal challenges (daytime or nighttime; immediate or deferred communication), and socio-economic, cultural, or political limitations (cf. Sykes, 2017, pp. 118-133; Warschauer, 1999; Warschauer & Kern, 2000). Moreover, the inherent characteristics of the computer as a technological tool have led to an exploration of the multifaceted dimensions of CALL, succinctly articulated in what Egbert (2005, p. 5) termed "the CALL equation." As described in Figure 7, the factor of 'context' is closely linked to other key factors such as affordances, pedagogical tasks, and the interaction between a teacher and learners.

learners (with their thoughts, behaviors, motivations, experiences, and understandings)
+ **language** (including its status and structure)
+ **context** (physical and temporal environment and the social, economic, cultural, and linguistic influences)
+ **one or more tools** (and the affordances the tool provides)
+ **tasks/activities** (content, structure, and organization)
+/– **peers and teachers** or others who can affect the process

= CALL

Figure 7. "The CALL equation" replicated from Egbert (2005, p. 5)

The scope of CALL's multidimensionality has expanded alongside advancements in digital technology, facilitating global connectivity through transitions from wired to wireless internet, and subsequently advancing into mobile technology in the early 2000s (cf. Kukulska-Hulme, Lee, & Norris, 2017). The broadening of dimensions is clearly reflected in the titles of publications by leading CALL researchers, as presented in Table 1, spanning from the 1990s to the early 2000s.

Table 1. Publications by leading CALL researchers from the 1990s to the early 2000s

Titles of the publications	Authors
The power of CALL	Pennington (1996b)
Technology-enhanced language learning	Bush & Terry (1997)
Electronic literacies: Language, culture, and power in online education	Warschauer (1999)
Network-based language teaching: Concepts and practice	Warschauer & Kern (2000)
Computer applications in second language acquisition: Foundations for teaching, testing and research	Chapelle (2001)
New perspectives on CALL for second language classrooms	Fotos & Browne (2004)
CALL dimensions: Options and issues in Computer-Assisted Language Learning	Levy & Stockwell (2006)

In light of the historical development along with the technological advancements, as well as the conceptual and pedagogical progression, the multidimensionality of CALL can be graphically summarized. As presented in Figure 8, it is conceptualized from CALL 1.0 to CALL 3.0.

CALL 1.0 characterizes the initial stage in which the potential of computers for L2 education began to be recognized. Significant advancements in hardware were achieved during

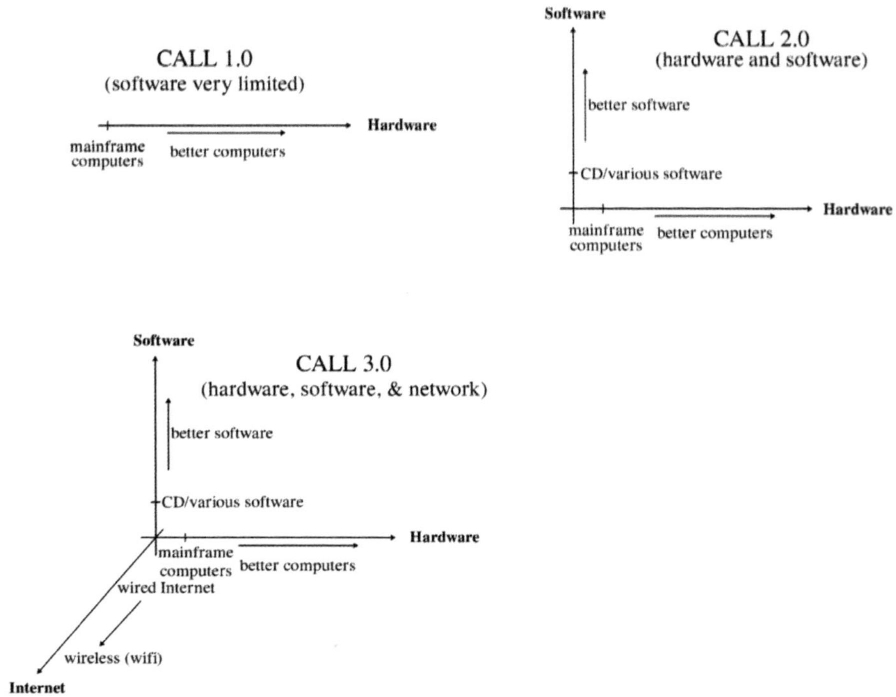

Figure 8. The multidimensionality of CALL: From CALL 1.0 to CALL 3.0

the 1970s, despite the constraints posed by software limitations and the restricted accessibility for L2 educators and learners. In the subsequent phase, termed CALL 2.0, the evolution of software was closely integrated with continued hardware developments throughout the late 1980s and 1990s, highlighting the increasing potential of CALL. CALL 3.0 further extended these developments, transforming the existing dimensions into more complex, multidimensional environments supported by ubiquitous networks from the mid-1990s to the 2010s. As Otto (2017, p. 20) noted, computer technology has become "a normal part of everyday practice" in L2 education. Furthermore, the integration of this technology has increased the critical importance of "context" for the efficacy of CALL (Egbert, 2005, p. 4).

The rise of generative AI, increasingly integrated into L2 education and introducing new contextual challenges for teachers and learners, necessitates a reassessment of the existing CALL 3.0 framework (cf. Godwin-Jones, 2024; KATE, 2023, 2024; KOSETA, 2024; Pack & Maloney, 2023, 2024; Shin & Lee, 2023; Warschauer & Xu, 2024). The reassessment seeks to incorporate the unique features that generative AI brings to L2 education. For example, ChatGPT and other LLMs exhibit linguistic capabilities comparable to native English speakers in ESL education – a phenomenon previously unobserved and unaccounted for within both historical and current CALL frameworks. Consequently, the impact of ChatGPT on ESL education could be more significant and immediate than in any other academic fields. Indeed, "[w]e are at a critical juncture in considering the role of [AI] in language learning" (Warschauer & Xu, 2024, p. 1). This situation demands a reconceptualization of various aspects of ESL education, including teacher roles, instructional methodologies, material development, assessment design, and teacher education, to name but a few.

From the CALL 1.0 through the CALL 3.0 framework, computer technology is viewed as an instructional tool. With the introduction of generative AI, however, it is more likely to be redefined as an instructional agent for ESL learners, potentially assuming responsibilities traditionally held by ESL instructors (Fathi & Rahimi, 2024; Wang & Gayed, 2024). Such a pivotal change suggests that generative AI could profoundly transform established instructional structures and the teacher-student dynamic that has long characterized language education (cf. Else, 2023; Pack & Maloney, 2024; Takahashi, 2023; Warschauer & Xu, 2024).

Human language has long been regarded as the final bastion that distinguishes humans from computers, due to its inherent complexity that machines can neither perfectly replicate nor even rudimentarily imitate. As a result, it is widely held that no technological tool can substitute for ESL teachers in aiding learners to achieve accuracy and fluency in English speaking and writing. Upon observing the remarkable capabilities of ChatGPT in human language, particularly, in English, and analyzing its internal mechanisms, Wolfram (2023) puts forth a compelling speculation.

> In other words, the reason a neural net can be successful in writing an essay is because writing an essay turns out to be a "computationally shallower" problem than we thought. And in a sense this takes us close to "having a theory" of how humans manage to do things like writing essays, or in general deal with language. (p. 57, quotation marks in original)

Should human language prove simpler to represent via computational means than previously assumed, it is anticipated that the proficiency of computers in emulating human language will significantly improve in the forthcoming years (cf. Blackford & Broderick, 2014; Bostrom, 2014; Kurzweil, 2005). Irrespective of the accuracy of Wolfram's hypothesis, the current empirical evidence indicates that ChatGPT exhibits exceptional performance (e.g., Alexander, 2024; Else, 2023; Fathi & Rahimi, 2024; Heaven, 2023a; Hutson, 2024; Omar et al., 2024; Pack & Maloney, 2023; Wang & Gayed, 2024). This compels ESL professionals to revisit a crucial question: Can the exceptional performance of ChatGPT be a benefit or a risk in ESL education?

Given the historical advancements in CALL, both technological and pedagogical, generative AI is expected to continue improving in its handling of human language with enhanced accuracy and fluency. As a result, it is likely to become an integral part of ESL teaching and learning environments, both within and beyond the classroom, as has been the case with previous CALL technologies. In such an instance, however, the role it is poised to assume extends beyond that of a mere technological tool, positioning it instead as an agent comparable to a teacher (Fridman, 2024; Godwin-Jones, 2024; Heikkilä, 2024d, Patel, 2023; Russell & Norvig, 2021, pp. 31-34; Sutskever, 2023).

In light of this development, critical considerations must be addressed regarding the deployment of teacher-like AI. Foremost among these is the ethical facet, focusing particularly on the implications for L2 learners rather than L2 teachers. Due to its impact on L2 learners, the teacher-like AI agent must be rigorously evaluated on its effectiveness and potential impacts, thereby categorizing it as either beneficial, detrimental or perhaps somewhere in between (Godwin-Jones, 2024; Johnson, 2023).

The longstanding debate about the dual nature of AI, which dates back to the early stages of AI development, centers on whether AI will ultimately prove beneficial or harmful. Searl (1980) explored the antithetical features through the characterization of "weak AI" and "strong AI":

> According to weak AI, the principal value of the computer in the study of the mind is that it gives us a very powerful tool. ··· But according to strong AI the computer is not merely a tool in the study of the mind; rather, the appropriately programmed computer *is* a mind, in the sense that computers given the right programs can be literally said to *understand* and have other cognitive states.
>
> (p. 417, italic in original)

Reflecting on the potential dangers associated with the power of strong AI, Bengio (2023) provided an analytical discussion on "rogue AI," defined as "an autonomous AI system that could behave in ways that would be catastrophically harmful to a large fraction of humans." He suggested that the most likely manifestations of such AIs are "goal-driven AI systems," programmed to pursue specific objectives without "limiting their agency." Further, he noted that "current LLMs have little or no agency but could be transformed into goal-driven AI systems." Along similar lines, Russell and Norvig (2010) highlighted ethical issues at opposite ends of the AI spectrum, from weak AI to strong AI:

> Most AI researchers take the weak AI hypothesis for granted, and don't care about the strong AI hypothesis—as long as their program works, they don't care whether you call it a simulation of intelligence or real intelligence. All AI researchers should be concerned with the ethical implications of their work. (p. 1020)

The point raised by Russell and Norvig (2010) parallels the concerns of ESL professionals who also face ethical challenges when engaging with AI technologies (cf. Godwin-Jones, 2024).

As discussed earlier, ChatGPT can enhance its performance through 'few-shot learning' (i.e., providing a few examples within the prompt) and 'in-context learning' (i.e., learning from the broader context provided within a single prompt) (Brown et al., 2020; Frank, 2023; Zhao et al., 2024). These approaches are integral to 'prompt engineering,' the practice of designing prompts to effectively guide LLMs (cf. Ahmed, 2024; Bsharat, Myrzakhan, & Shen, 2024; Kim & Park, 2024; Ozdemir, 2023, pp. 57-67). The prompt engineering is considered critical for the successful use of ChatGPT by a wide range of users, including ESL teachers and learners (e.g., Wang & Greyed, 2024). The central aspects of few-shot learning and in-context learning emphasize the importance of human interaction in refining ChatGPT's capabilities, in much the same way as the dynamics of L2 learning. Interactions are vital for improving LLMs' precision in understanding input and addressing complex challenges, drawing parallels with the issues thoroughly examined by the interaction (cf. Gass & Mackey, 2006; Hall, 2010; Long, 1983a, 1983b) and sociocultural perspectives in L2 learning (cf. Johnson, 2004; Lantolf & Beckett, 2009).

Considering that ChatGPT generates more effective outputs through interactions with ESL learners, it is imperative for ESL educators to carefully evaluate whether its use is advantageous or potentially harmful in specific instructional contexts. At present, ChatGPT is generally considered to be a "weak AI," serving primarily as an advanced teaching and learning tool (Searl, 1980, p. 417). However, within a certain ESL learning environment, the impact of this tool can vary, as learners may employ it either constructively or detrimentally based on their intentions. Accordingly, even though ChatGPT is currently recognized as weak AI, it has the potential to function as either *conformable AI* or *recalcitrant AI*, contingent upon its application within the ESL context.

The former, similar to previous CALL technologies, represents AI functioning as an assisting tool: for teachers, it aids in improving instructional processes from design to assessment; for learners, it enhances the effectiveness of their learning experiences. Conversely, the latter depicts AI as a replacement for ESL teachers, acting as a teaching agent that replicates the role of an ESL instructor in situations where the responsibilities and accountabilities of such a teacher-like role are neither clearly defined nor thoroughly discussed. For learners, this type of AI may be misused, whether intentionally or unintentionally. Godwin-Jones (2024, p. 13), focusing solely on the context of writing assignments, clearly describe the potential risks of recalcitrant AI for L2 learners, noting that "AI offers many potential benefits, but also concerns, as instructors fear students will simply turn over [all assignments] to AI to complete."

In fact, an increasing number of studies demonstrate the efficacy of AI in L2 teaching and learning (cf. Fathi &

Rahimi, 2024; Lee & Lee, 2024; Shin & Lee, 2023; Woo et al., 2024). As L2 learners become aware of the effectiveness and convenience of AI-guided learning, they may begin to rely more heavily on AI than on their instructors – a shift not observed with previous CALL technologies. This leads to an essential inquiry: Could this trend signal the onset of teacher replacement by AI? Moreover, the use of AI as recalcitrant AI by L2 learners is often imperceptible to L2 educators, thereby complicating efforts to manage its impact. In line with Godwin-Jones' (2024, p. 13) concerns, the potential for negative outcomes increases if learners "simply turn over" their tasks and assignments (e.g., writing, grammar practice, reading comprehension questions) "to AI to complete," thereby fostering an over-reliance on AI.

What measures should be taken when confronted with a replicant AI teacher whose proficiency either matches or surpasses that of a human ESL educator? Reflecting on Chapelle's (2001, p. 1) comments, it will become necessary to initially address the question of whether a replicant AI teacher "*should* be used" before considering how a replicant AI teacher "can best be used." If the relevance of the latter inquiry proliferates, one might then question the continued necessity of human teachers. Moreover, as Otto (2017, p. 20) has highlighted, what implications would arise if replicant AI teachers remain constant in presence but evolves in format and capability, eventually becoming "a normal part of everyday practice" in all aspects of future ESL education? The human-like AI teacher "may initially be developed by humans, but as it grows it follows its own path, going where no human has gone before – and where no human can follow" (Harari, 2017, p. 458).

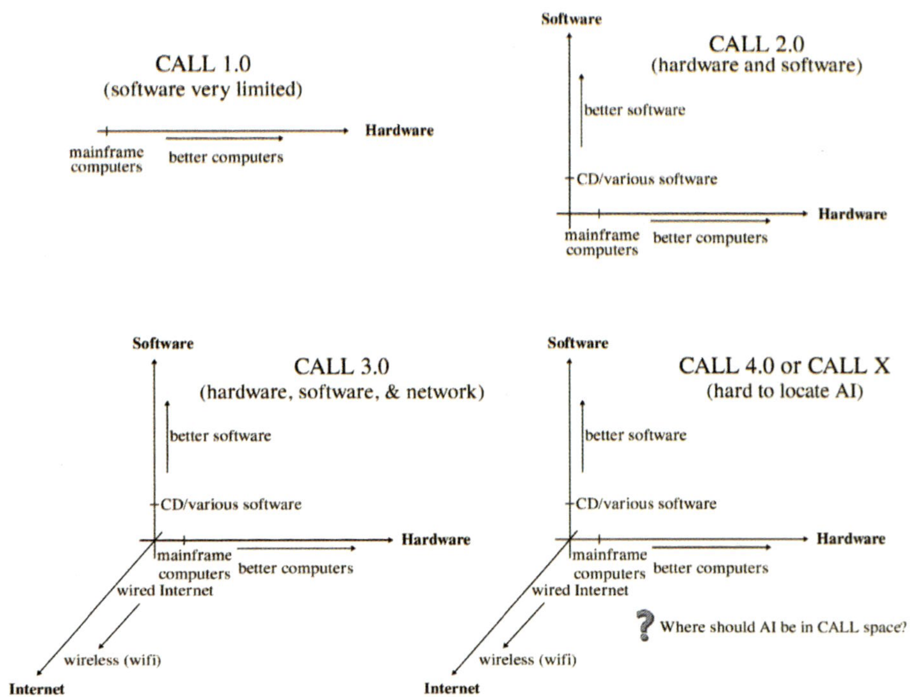

Figure 9. Emerging dimensions of AI in CALL 3.0: Toward CALL 4.0 or CALL X

The potential for unexpected and previously unencountered scenarios can be attributed to the introduction of an obscure and enigmatic dimension of AI within CALL, which extends more broadly to the field of ESL education. Such development may require ESL professionals to adopt novel conceptual and instructional strategies to effectively tackle these challenges. As Lanier (Bloomberg Originals, 2023, 3:35-3:39) articulates, "to be an optimist, you have to have the courage to be a fearsome critic" when integrating AI technology. As depicted in Figure 9, the future trajectory of CALL could diverge significantly depending on the efficacy with which these new AI-related challenges are addressed. Specifically, this could result in the evolution of CALL into either *CALL 4.0*, where AI technologies enhance the richness and efficacy of L2 research and instruction, making it more conceptually and pedagogically robust, or *CALL X*, where the AI technology could lead to CALL becoming lost and conceptually and pedagogically deprived due to AI's capacity to autonomously manage all aspects of L2 learning.

Conclusion

"Fei-Fei, what *else* can AI do to help people?"
– Fei-Fei's mom –
(Li, 2023, p. 243, italic in original)

This book explores the evolution of AI, both conceptually and technologically, across the century. It also delves into ChatGPT's fundamental mechanisms and features tailored to ESL professionals, and then addresses generative AI within the framework of CALL in ESL education. Specifically, the findings from the exploration are summarized in two main points.

First, the historical review of AI development suggests that, despite numerous obstacles, the recent achievements of ChatGPT and other generative AI variants have been realized through 'the stream of artificial consciousness' – the pertinacious endeavor by AI researchers to computationally create machines that can think and process emotions like the human mind – over the century. Second, the manner in which ChatGPT processes information conceptually mirrors that of the human brain. In other words, the resemblance is computationally represented, analogous to key aspects of L2 learning process, such as the 'negotiation of meaning' in a communication between a teacher and learners, 'attention' in the Noticing Hypothesis, and the importance of language input in both quantity and quality. Additionally, ChatGPT demonstrates remarkable performance despite being less complex than the human brain.

The exceptional performance of ChatGPT and its relevance to ESL education necessitate a critical reevaluation of the current

CALL framework. Such a reevaluation should incorporate previously unconsidered and emerging dimensions that ChatGPT has introduced to the field, thereby facilitating the integration of generative AI into ESL pedagogy. A thorough reassessment will foster more informed and inclusive CALL frameworks that comprehensively address myriad issues associated with generative AI, including its potential benefits and drawbacks, its role in enhancing agency within ESL education, and the ethical implications it raises.

While "how far the current wave of excitement will go is anybody's guess," it is anticipated that generative AI will become an integral part of ESL education in the near future, as supported by the historical trajectory of AI and CALL development (Bostrom, 2014, p. 322). Historically, ESL educators have alternated between traditional teaching methods and innovative approaches with the introduction of new technologies, such as the integration of computers into ESL instruction. Currently, they find themselves at a critical juncture: they must decide whether to advance ESL education with the beneficial features of AI, termed *CALL 4.0*, or to contend with a version of ESL education that fails to fully realize the benefits of AI, hence presenting significant challenges, referred to as *CALL X*.

Resolving these emerging issues effectively depends not solely on AI technology but on the adeptness of ESL professionals. Specifically, ESL professionals need to carefully contemplate the significant outperformance of generative AI and even its potential for super-performance. Refined approaches to ChatGPT, informed by the reassessment of CALL, will empower ESL educators to employ AI more strategically and effectively in their instructional methodologies.

References

60 Minutes. (2023a, October 9). *"Godfather of AI" Geoffrey Hinton: The 60 Minutes interview* [Video]. YouTube. https://www.youtube.com/watch?v=qrvK_KuIeJk

60 Minutes. (2023b, December 30). *Artificial intelligence | 60 Minutes full episodes* [Video]. YouTube. https://www.youtube.com/watch?v=aZ5EsdnpLMI

60 Minutes. (2024, April 29). *Nvidia CEO Jensen Huang and the $2 trillion company powering today's AI | 60 Minutes* [Video]. YouTube. https://www.youtube.com/watch?v=DpQQi2scsHo

Abbott, L. F., Losonczy, A., & Sawtell, N. B. (2021). The computational bases of neural circuits that mediate behavior. In E. R. Kandel, J. H. Schwartz, T. M. Jessell, S. A. Siegelbaum, & A. J., Hudspeth (Eds.), *Principles of neural science* (6th ed.) (pp. 97-110). McGraw Hill/Medical.

Adams, J. (2024). *AI foundations of neural networks*. Green Mountain Computing.
https://a.co/d/0dqvrLXV

Agar, J. (2020). What is science for? The Lighthill report on artificial intelligence reinterpreted, *The British Journal for the History of Science, 53*(3), 289-310. https://doi.org/10.1017/S0007087420000230

Aggarwal, C. C. (2023). *Neural networks and deep learning* (2nd ed.). Springers.

AI winter. (2024, May 1). In *Wikipedia*.
https://en.wikipedia.org/w/index.php?title=AI_winter&action=history

Alexander, D. (2024, April 16). Why ChatGPT-4's score on the bar exam may not be so impressive. *New York State Bar Association*. https://nysba.org/why-gpt-4s-score-on-the-bar-exam-may-not-be-so-impressive

Amanpour and Company. (2023, May 10). *"Godfather of AI" Geoffrey Hinton warns of the "existential threat" of AI* [Video]. YouTube.

https://www.youtube.com/watch?v=Y6Sgp7y178k

Ananthaswamy, A. (2023). In AI, is bigger better? *Nature, 615,* 202-205. https://www.nature.com/articles/d41586-023-00641-w

Anyoha, R. (2017, August 28). The history of Artificial Intelligence. *Science in the News.* https://sitn.hms.harvard.edu/flash/2017/history-artificial-intelligence

Apple Machine Learning Research. (2024, June 10). *Introducing Apple's on-device and server foundation models.* https://machinelearning.apple.com/research/introducing-apple-foundation-models

Arts & Science – University of Toronto. (2024, February 24). *Geoffrey Hinton in conversation with Fei-Fei Li — Responsible AI development* [Video]. YouTube. https://www.youtube.com/watch?v=QWWgr2rN45o

B10NUMB3RS. (n.d.). *Diameter of human hair.* https://bionumbers.hms.harvard.edu/bionumber.aspx?id=106856&ver=2

Bajaj, S. (2024, June 7). This AI-powered "black box" could make surgery safer. *MIT Technology Review,* https://www.technologyreview.com/2024/06/07/1093338/surgical-safety-technologies-ai-black-box-surgery-operating-room

Barrett, L. F. (2020). *Seven and a half lessons about the brain.* Mariner Books. https://a.co/d/bMYNM8H

BBC News. (2023, May 2). *AI 'godfather' quits Google over dangers of Artificial Intelligence - BBC News* [Video]. YouTube. https://www.youtube.com/watch?v=DsBGaHywRhs

Bengio, Y. (2023, May 22). How rogue AIs may arise. *Yoshua Bengio.* https://yoshuabengio.org/2023/05/22/how-rogue-ais-may-arise

Bengio, Y., LeCun, Y., & Hinton, G. (2021). Deep learning for AI. *Communications of the ACM, 84*(7), 58-65. https://doi.org/10.1145/3448250

Bennett, M. (2023). *A brief history of intelligence: Evolution, AI, and the five breakthroughs that made our brains.* Mariner Books. https://a.co/d/

azU9HHs

Berkman Klein Center. (2019, October 11). *Ethics and governance of AI at Berkman Klein: Report on impact, 2017-2019*. https://cyber.harvard.edu/story/2019-10/ethics-and-governance-ai-berkman-klein-report-impact-2017-2019

Bernstein, J. (1981, December 6). Profiles: A.I. *The New Yorker*. https://www.newyorker.com/magazine/1981/12/14/a-i

Bernstein, D. A., Penner, L. A., Clarke-Stewart, A., & Roy, E. J. (2006). *Psychology* (7th ed.) (Revised special edition for the Ohio State University). Houghton Mifflin Company.

Biber, D., & Conrad, S. (2009). *Register, genre, and style*. Cambridge University Press.

Biber, D., Connor, U., & Upton, T. A. (2007). *Discourse on the move: Using corpus analysis to describe discourse structure*. John Benjamins Publishing Company.

Bishop, C. M, & Bishop, H. (2023). *Deep learning Foundations and concepts*. Springers.

Blackford, R., & Broderick, D. (Eds.) (2014). *Intelligence unbound: The future of uploaded and machine minds*. Wiley Blackwell.

Bloomberg Originals. (2023, November 16). *Jaron Lanier Looks into AI's Future | AI IRL* [Video]. YouTube. https://www.youtube.com/watch?v=o8vU9QtcMZw

Boas, M. L. (2006). *Mathematical methods in the physical sciences* (3rd ed.). Wiley.

Boston Dynamics. (2024, April 17). *All new Atlas* [Video]. YouTube. https://www.youtube.com/watch?v=29ECwExc _M

Bostrom, N. (2014). *Superintelligence: Paths, Dangers, Strategies*. Oxford University Press.

Bove, T. (2023, February 3). The A.I. revolution is here: ChatGPT could be the fastest-growing app in history and more than half of traders say it could disrupt investing the most. *Fortune*. https://fortune.com/2023/02/02/chatgpt-fastest-growing-app-in-history-could-revolutionize-trading

Branch Education. (2023, December 12). *How do video game graphics work?* [Video]. YouTube. https://www.youtube.com/watch?v=C8YtdC8mxTU

Bridgman, P. W. (1927). *The logic of modern physics*. The Macmillan Company.

Brown, C. E., & O'Leary, D. E. (1994, December 17). *Introduction to artificial intelligence and expert systems*. https://msbfile03.usc.edu/digitalmeasures/doleary/intellcont/Brown-Oleary-es_tutor-1.htm

Brown, H. D. (2006). *Principles of language teaching and learning* (5th ed.). Pearson.

Brown, T. B., Mann, B., Ryder, N., Subbiah, M., Kaplan, J., Dhariwal, P., Neelakantan, A., Shyam, P., Sastry, G., Askell, A., Agarwal, S., Herbert-Voss, A., Krueger, G., Henighan, T., Child, R., Ramesh, A., Ziegler, D. M., Wu, J., Winter, Cl., Hesse, C., Chen, M., Sigler, E., Litwin, M., Gray, S., Chess, B., Clark, J., Berner, C., McCandlish, S., Radford, A., Sutskever, I., & Amodei, D. (2020). *Language models are few-shot learners*. arXive. https://doi.org/10.48550/arXiv.2005.14165

Brysbaert, M., & Rastle, K. (2009). *Historical and conceptual issues in psychology*. Pearson Education Limited.

Bsharat, S. M., Myrzakhan, A., & Shen, Z. (2024). *Principled instructions are all you need for questioning LLaMA-1/2, GPT-3.5/4*. arXive. https://doi.org/10.48550/arXiv.2312.16171

Buduma, N., Buduma, N., & Papa, J. (2022). *Fundamentals of Deep Learning: Designing Next-Generation Machine Intelligence Algorithms* (2nd ed.). O'Reilly Media.
https://a.co/d/gnzFtZF

Bush, M. D., & Terry, R. M. (Eds.) (1997). *Technology-enhanced language learning*.
National Textbook Company.

Cachat-Rosset, G., & Klarsfeld, A. (2023). Diversity, equity, and inclusion in artificial intelligence: An evaluation of guidelines. *Applied Artificial Intelligence, 37*(1). https://doi.org/10.1080/08839514.2023.2176618

Carrell, P. L., Devine, J., & Eskey, D. E. (Eds.) (1998). *Interactive approaches to second language reading*. Cambridge University Press.

Castellan, C. (2024, April 10). If big techs are all buying the entire LLM markets, is there any space left for startups? *Medium*. https://medium.com/b8125-spring2024/if-big-techs-are-all-buying-the-entire-llm-market-is-there-any-space-left-for-startups-66e16daec9ae

Caulfield, B. (2009, December 16). What's the difference between a CPU and a GPU? *nVIDIA*. https://blogs.nvidia.com/blog/whats-the-difference-between-a-cpu-and-a-gpu

CBS Mornings. (2023a, March 25). *Full interview: "Godfather of artificial intelligence" talks impact and potential of AI* [Video]. YouTube. https://www.youtube.com/watch?v=qpoRO378qRY

CBS Mornings. (2023b, December 16). *Meta's Chief AI Scientist Yann LeCun talks about the future of artificial intelligence* [Video]. YouTube. https://www.youtube.com/watch?v=Ah6nR8YAYF4

Center for AI Safety. (n.d.). *Statement of AI risk: Sign the statement.* https://www.safe.ai/work/statement-on-ai-risk#open-letter

Chapelle, C. A. (2001). *Computer applications in second language acquisition: Foundations for teaching, testing and research*. Cambridge University Press.

Chapelle, C. A. (2003). *English language learning and technology*. John Benjamins Publishing Company.

Chen, S. (2024, June 5). How a simple circuit could offer an alternative to energy-intensive GPUs. *MIT Technology Review*, https://www.technologyreview.com/2024/06/05/1093250/how-a-simple-circuit-could-offer-an-alternative-to-energy-intensive-gpus

Choi, Y. (2022). The curious case of commonsense intelligence. *Daedalus, 151*(2),

139-155. https://doi.org/10.1162/daed_a_01906

Choi, Y. (2023, April). *Why AI is incredibly smart and shockingly stupid* [Video]. TED Conferences. https://www.ted.com/talks/yejin_choi_why_ai_is_incredibly_smart_and_shockingly_stupid/c?language=en

Chomsky, N. (1968). *Language and mind.* Harcourt Brace Jovanovich.

Chomsky, N., Roberts, I., & Watumull, J. (2023, March 8). Noam Chomsky: The false promise of ChatGPT. *The New York Times,* online. https://www.nytimes.com/2023/03/08/opinion/noam-chomsky-chatgpt-ai.html?searchResultPosition=1

Chun, D. M., & Plass, J. L. (1996). Effects of multimedia annotations on vocabulary acquisition. *Modern Language Journal, 80*(2), 183-198.

CNBC. (2023, March 6). *How Nvidia grew from gaming to A.I. giant, now powering ChatGPT* [Video]. YouTube. https://www.youtube.com/watch?v=d3L2uPuxOxU

CNBC. (2024a, July 9). *Why Nvidia, Tesla, Amazon and more are betting big on AI-powered humanoid robots* [Video]. YouTube. https://www.youtube.com/watch?v=v0uKLCZocjs

CNBC. (2024b, July 29). *How the massive power draw of generative AI is overtaxing our grid* [Video]. YouTube. https://www.youtube.com/watch?v=MJQIQJYxey4

Coeckelbergh, M. (2020). *AI ethics.* The MIT Press. https://a.co/d/gbrIo47

Cohen, J. (1968). Multiple regression as a general data-analytic system. *Psychological Bulletin, 70*(6), 426-443.

Coltri, M. A. (2024). The ethical dilemma with Open AI ChatGPT: Is it right or wrong to prohibit it? *Athens Journal of Law, 10*(1), 119-130. https://doi.org/10.30958/ajl.10-1-6

Cook, V. (1983). Chomsky's universal grammar and second language learning. *Applied Linguistics, 6*(1), 2-18.

Corbett, J. J., & Chen, J. (2017). The visual system. In D. E. Haines & G. A.

Mihailoff (Eds.), *Fundamental neuroscience for basic and clinical applications* (5th ed.) (pp. 286-305). Elsevier. https://a.co/d/0iAmFIsW

Crick, F. (1995). *The astonishing hypothesis: The scientific search for the soul.* Scribner.

Crossley, S. A., Allen, D., & McNamara, D. S. (2012). Text simplification and comprehensible input: A case for an intuitive approach. *Language Research Teaching*, 16(1), 89-108.

Cybenko, G. (1989). Approximation by superpositions of a sigmoidal function. *Math. Control Signal Systems, 2,* 303-314. https://doi.org/10.1007/BF02551274

Dante, J. (Director). (1987). *Innerspace* [Film]. Warner Bros.

Darthmouth workshop. (2024, April 12). In *Wikipedia.* https://en.wikipedia.org/wiki/Dartmouth_workshop

David, B. (Writer), Weiss, D. B. (Writer), & Patten, T. V. (Director). (2011, April 17). Winter is coming (Season 1, Episode 1) [TV series episode]. In D. Benioff & D. B. Weiss (Executive Producers), *Game of Thrones.* HBO.

Davis, C. R., & Squire, P. (2023, June 4). Air Force colonel backtracks over his warning about how AI could go rogue and kill its human operators. *Business Insider.* https://www.businessinsider.com/ai-powered-drone-tried-killing-its-operator-in-military-simulation-2023-6

Dechter, R. (1986). Learning while searching in constraint-satisfaction-problems. *AAAI-86 Proceedings*, 178-183. https://cdn.aaai.org/AAAI/1986/AAAI86-029.pdf

Dennett, D. C. (1981). *Brainstorms: Philosophical essays on mind and psychology.* The MIT Press. (Original work published 1978)

Diakopoulos, N. (2020). Transparency. In M. D. Dubber, F. Pasquale, & S. Das (Eds.), *The Oxford handbook of ethics of AI.* (pp.197-213). Oxford University Press. https://a.co/d/7jDMrif

Dignum, V. (2020). Responsibility and artificial intelligence. In M. D. Dubber, F. Pasquale, & S. Das (Eds.), *The Oxford handbook of ethics of AI.* (pp.215-231). Oxford University Press.
https://a.co/d/7jDMrif

Duarte, F. (2024, April 30). Number of ChatGPT users. *Exploding Topics.* https://explodingtopics.com/blog/chatgpt-users

Eagleman, D. (2015). *The brain: The story of you.* Vintage. https://a.co/d/01ZcBv5M

Egbert, J. (2005). Conducting research on CALL. In J. Egbert & G. M. Petrie (Eds.), *CALL research perspectives* (pp. 3-8). Lawrence Erlbaum Associates.

Ellis, N., & Collins, L. (2009). Input and second language acquisition: The roles of frequency, form, and function. Introduction to the special issue. *Modern Language Journal, 93*(3), 329-335.

Ellis, R. (1993). The structural syllabus and second language acquisition. *TESOL Quarterly, 27*(1), 91-113.

Ellis, R. (1994). *The study of second language acquisition.* Oxford University Press.

Else, H. (2023). Abstracts written by ChatGPT fool scientists. *Nature, 613*, 423. https://www.nature.com/articles/d41586-023-00056-7

Ervin, D. H., & Valentine, J. W. (2013). *The Cambrian explosion: The construction of animal biodiversity.* Roberts and Company Publishers

Eye on AI. (2023. November 2). *Yann LeCun on world models, AI threats and open-sourcing* [Video].
YouTube. https://www.youtube.com/watch?v=vjrU4MWjd6Y

Fathi, J., & Rahimi, M. (2024). Utilizing artificial intelligence-enhanced writing mediation to develop academic writing skills in EFL learners: a qualitative study. *Computer Assisted Language Learning,* 1-40. https://doi.org/10.1080/09588221.2024.2374772

Faust, J. (2023, January 11). Fun with OpenAI, medical charting, and diagnostics. (Also: I just got lied to by a bot). *Inside Medicine.* https://insidemedicine.

substack.com/p/fun-with-openai-medical-charting

Fetch.ai. (2024a, March 15). History of AI: Part three – AI winter (70s). *Medium.* https://medium.com/fetch-ai/history-of-ai-part-three-ai-winter-1970s-fc52b3130f27

Fetch.ai. (2024b, March 20). History of AI: Part four – The boom (80s). *Medium.* https://medium.com/fetch-ai/history-of-ai-part-iv-the-boom-80s-1e45b1d9ec91

Fetch.ai. (2024c, April 4). History of AI: Part five – The expansion (90s). *Medium.* https://medium.com/fetch-ai/history-of-ai-part-five-the-expansion-90s-c6cb1662603e

Fotos, S. (2001). Cognitive approaches to grammar instruction. In M. Celce-Murcia (Ed.), *Teaching English as a second or foreign language* (3rd ed.) (pp. 267-284). Heinle & Heinle.

Fotos, S., & Browne, C. M. (Eds.) (2004). *New perspectives on CALL for second language classrooms.* Lawrence Erlbaum Associates.

Fridman, L. (2020. March 1). *John Hopfield: Physics View of the Mind and Neurobiology | Lex Fridman Podcast #76* [Video]. YouTube. https://www.youtube.com/watch?v=DKyzcbNr8WE

Fridman, L. (2024. March 8). *Yann LeCun: Meta AI, open source, limits of LLMs, AGI & the future of AI | Lex Fridman Podcast #416* [Video]. YouTube. https://www.youtube.com/watch?v=5t1vTLU7s40

Frank, M. C. (2023). Bridging the data gap between children and large language models. *Trends in Cognitive Science, 27*(11), 990-992. https://doi.org/10.1016/j.tics.2023.08.007

Friedenberg, J. (2010). *Artificial psychology: The quest for what it means to be human.* Psychology Press. https://a.co/d/35L80VJ

Gabriel, I., & Ghazavi, V. (2023). The challenge of value alignment: From fairer algorithms to AI safety. In C. Véliz (Ed.), *The Oxford handbook of digital ethics.* (pp.336-355). Oxford University Press. https://a.co/d/6i2W2X8

Gardner, E. P., & Johnson, K. O. (2013). Sensory coding. In E. R. Kandel, J. H.

Schwartz, T. M. Jessell, S. A. Siegelbaum, & A. J. Hudspeth (Eds.), *Principles of neural science* (5th ed.) (pp. 1307-1372). McGraw Hill/Medical.

Gass, S., & Mackey, A. (2006). Input, interaction and output: An overview. In K. Bardovi-Harlig & Z. Dörnyei (Eds.), *AILA review: Themes in SLA research (Volume 19)*. (pp. 3-17). John Benjamins Publishing Company.

Gleitman, L. R., Newport, E .L., & Gleitman, H. (1984). The current status of the motherese hypothesis. *Journal of Child Language, 11*(1), 43-79.

Glover, E. (2023, April 21). What is AI winter? *builtin*. https://builtin.com/artificial-intelligence/ai-winter

Godwin-Jones, R. (2024). Distributed agency in language learning and teaching through generative AI. *Language Learning & Technology, 28*(2), 5–31. https://hdl.handle.net/10125/73570

Goodfellow, I., Bengio, Y., & Courville, A. (2016). *Deep learning*. The MIT Press. https://a.co/d/cPEVphx

Gottfredson, L. S. (1997). Mainstream science on intelligence: An editorial with 52 signatories, history, and bibliography, *INTELLIGENCE, 24*(1), 13-23.

Gould, S. J. (1996). *The mismeasure of man*. W. W. Norton & Company. (Original work published 1981).

Grabe, W. (2009). *Reading in a second language: Moving from theory to practice*. Cambridge University Press.

Grabe, W., & Stoller, F. L. (2002). *Teaching and researching reading*. Longman.

Grattarola, F. (2018, December 15). Rina Dechter – Deep learning pioneer. *Medium*.
https://medium.com/a-computer-of-ones-own/rina-dechter-deep-learning-pioneer-e7e9ccc96c6e

Gunderson, K. (1985). *Mentality and machines* (2nd ed.). University of Minnesota Press. (Original work published 1971)

Haenlein, M., & Kaplan, A. (2019). A brief history of artificial intelligence: On the past, present, and future of Artificial Intelligence [Special Issue on AI]. *California Management Review, 61*(4), 5-14. https://doi.

org/10.1177/0008125619864925

Hall, J. K. (2010). Interaction as method and result of language learning. *Language Teaching, 43*(2), 202-215.

Han, Z., Park, E. S., & Combs, C. (2008). Textual enhancement of input: Issues and possibilities. *Applied Linguistics, 29*(4), 597-618.

Harari, N. Y. (2017). *Homo Deus: A brief history of tomorrow*. Harper. https://a.co/d/axawRz2

Hayes, A. F. (2005). *Statistical methods for communication science*. Lawrence Erlbaum Associates, Inc.

Heaven, W. D. (2023a, April 6). ChatGPT is going to change education, not destroy it. *MIT Technology Review*, https://www.technologyreview.com/2023/04/06/1071059/chatgpt-change-not-destroy-education-openai

Heaven, W. D. (2023b, May 2). Geoffrey Hinton tells us why he's now scared of the tech he helped build. *MIT Technology Review*, https://www.technologyreview.com/2023/05/02/1072528/geoffrey-hinton-google-why-scared-ai

Heaven, W. D. (2024a, March 4). Large language models can do jaw-dropping things. But nobody knows exactly why. *MIT Technology Review*, https://www.technologyreview.com/2024/03/04/1089403/large-language-models-amazing-but-nobody-knows-why

Heaven, W. D. (2024b, June 18). Why does AI hallucinate? *MIT Technology Review*, https://www.technologyreview.com/2024/06/18/1093440/what-causes-ai-hallucinate-chatbots

Heaven, W. D. (2024c, July 10). What is AI? *MIT Technology Review*, https://www.technologyreview.com/2024/07/10/1094475/what-is-artificial-intelligence-ai-definitive-guide

Heaven, W. D. (2024d, October 8). Geoffrey Hinton, AI pioneer and figurehead of doomerism, wins Nobel Prize. *MIT Technology Review*, https://www.technologyreview.com/2024/10/08/1105221/geoffrey-hinton-just-won-the-nobel-prize-in-physics-for-his-work-on-machine-learning

Heikkilä, M. (2022a, November 14). We're getting a better idea of AI's true carbon footprint. *MIT Technology Review*, https://www.technologyreview.com/2022/11/14/1063192/were-getting-a-better-idea-of-ais-true-carbon-footprint

Heikkilä, M. (2022b, December 19). How to spot AI-generated text. *MIT Technology Review*, https://www.technologyreview.com/2022/12/19/1065596/how-to-spot-ai-generated-text

Heikkilä, M. (2024a, January 29). Dear Taylor Swift, we're sorry about those explicit deepfackes. *MIT Technology Review*, https://www.technologyreview.com/2024/01/29/1087376/dear-taylor-swift-were-sorry-about-those-explicit-deepfakes

Heikkilä, M. (2024b, June 4). What I learned from the UN's "AI for Good" summit. *MIT Technology Review*, https://www.technologyreview.com/2024/06/04/1093123/what-i-learned-from-the-uns-ai-for-good-summit

Heikkilä, M. (2024c, June 18). Meta has created a way to watermark AI-generated speech. *MIT Technology Review*, https://www.technologyreview.com/2024/06/18/1094009/meta-has-created-a-way-to-watermark-ai-generated-speech

Heikkilä, M. (2024d, July 5). What are AI agents? *MIT Technology Review*, https://www.technologyreview.com/2024/07/05/1094711/what-are-ai-agents

Heikkilä, M. (2024e, September 25). A tiny new open-source AI model performs as well as powerful big ones. *MIT Technology Review*, https://www.technologyreview.com/2024/09/25/1104465/a-tiny-new-open-source-ai-model-performs-as-well-as-powerful-big-ones

Hendrycks, D., Mazeika, M., & Woodside, T. (2023). An overview of catastrophic

AI risks. *arXiv*, https://arxiv.org/abs/2306.12001

Hesiod (2008). *Theogony and works and days* (M. L. West, Trans.). OUP Oxford. (Original work published in 730-700 BC) https://a.co/d/55uzgKo

Hoffmann, J., Borgeaud, S., Mensch, A., Buchatskaya, E., Cai, T., Rutherford, E., Casas, D. L., Hendricks, L. A., Welbl, J., Clark, A., Hennigan, T., Noland, E., Millican, K., Driessche, G., Damoc, B., Guy, A., Osindero, S., Simonyan, K., Elsen, E., Rae, J. W., Vinyals, O., & Sifre, L. (2022). *Training compute-optimal large language models*. arXive. https://doi.org/10.48550/arXiv.2203.15556

Hofstadter, D. R. & Sander, E. (2013). *Surfaces and essences: Analogy as the fuel and fire of thinking*. Basic Book. https://a.co/d/4asloKp

Holman, C. H., Hibbard, A., & Thrall, W. F. (1979). The stream. In E. R. Steinberg (Ed.), *The stream-of-consciousness technique in the modern novel*. (pp. 5-7). Kennikat Press Corp.

Hopfield, J. J. (1982). Neural networks and physical systems with emergent collective computational abilities. *Proceedings of the National Academy of Science, 79*(8), 2554-2558. https://www.pnas.org/doi/epdf/10.1073/pnas.79.8.2554

Hukuoka, S. (2009). *The world cannot be understood even if divided*. Kodansha. https://amzn.asia/d/9dTuZmY

Hutson, M. (2024, May 14). How does ChatGPT 'think'? Psychology and neuroscience crack open AI large language models. *Nature, 629*, 986-988. https://www.nature.com/articles/d41586-024-01314-y

IBM. (2024). *IBM Watson to watsonx*. https://www.ibm.com/watson

Institute for Advanced Study (n.d.). *John von Neumann: Life, work, and legacy*. Retrieved on June 30, 2024, from https://www.ias.edu/von-neumann

Jaeger, R. M. (1984). *Sampling in education and the social sciences*. Longman.

James, W. (1950). *The principles of psychology: Volume one*. Dover Publications, Inc. (Original work published 1890)

Johns, T. (1994). From printout to handout: grammar and vocabulary teaching in the context of data-driven learning. In T. Odlin (Ed.), *Perspectives on pedagogical grammar* (pp. 293-313). Cambridge University Press.

Johnson, A. (2023, Jan.). ChatGPT in schools: Here's where it's banned – And how it could potentially help students. *Forbes.* https://www.forbes.com/sites/ariannajohnson/2023/01/18/chatgpt-in-schools-heres-where-its-banned-and-how-it-could-potentially-help-students/?sh=2f9cddb46e2c

Johnson, M. (2004). *A philosophy of second language acquisition.* Yale University Press.

Kandel, E. R., Barres, B. A., & Hudspeth, A. J. (2013). Nerve cells, neural circuitry, and behavior. In E. R. Kandel, J. H. Schwartz, T. M. Jessell, S. A. Siegelbaum, & A. J. Hudspeth (Eds.), *Principles of neural science* (5th ed.) (pp. 190-237). McGraw Hill/Medical. https://a.co/d/0308pAyO

Kaplan, A. (2022). *Artificial intelligence, business and civilization: Our fate made in machines.* Routledge. https://a.co/d/9MiBhKy

Kaplan, J., McCandlish, S., Henighan, T., Brown, T. B., Chess, B., Child, R., Gray, S., Radford, A., Wu, J., & Amodei, D. (2020). Scaling laws for neural language models. *arXiv.* https://arxiv.org/abs/2001.08361v1

KATE. (2023). *English language education in the era of digital transformation: Opportunities, connectivity, and sustainability.* 2023 KATE (The Korea Association of Teachers of English), ETAK, GETA, KAMALL, KAPEE, KASEE, KEES, KOSETA, MEESO, & PKETA Joint International Conference (2023, July 6-8), Seoul, Korea.

KATE. (2024). *Back to basics in the age of AI: Balancing technology and traditional teaching methods.* 2024 KATE (The Korea Association of Teachers of English) International Conference (2024, July 5-6), Yeosu, Korea.

Keil, F. (2006). Cognitive science and cognitive development. In D. Kuhn & R. S. Siegler (Eds.), *Handbook of child psychology volume two: Cognition, perception, and language* (6th ed.) (pp. 609-635). John Wiley & Sons, Inc.

Kim, S., & Park, S. (2024, July 30). [Prompt engineering – Part 1] Maximizing the use of LLM with prompt design. *Upstage*. https://www.upstage.ai/feed/insight/prompt-engineering-guide-maximizing-the-use-of-llm-with-prompt-design

Kish, L. (1978). Chance, statistics, and statisticians. *Journal of the American Statistical Association, 73*(361), 1-6. https://doi.org/10.2307/2286508

Kleinman, Z. (2023, June 2). US Air Force denies AI drone attacked operator in test. *BBC*. https://www.bbc.com/news/technology-65789916

Knight, W. (2016, January 26). What Marvin Minsky still means for AI. *MIT Technology Review*. https://www.technologyreview.com/2016/01/26/163622/what-marvin-minsky-still-means-for-ai

Koch, C. (2019). *The feeling of life itself: Why consciousness Is widespread but can't be computed*. The MIT Press. https://a.co/d/2mXhqnh

KOSETA. (2024). *Unleashing potential: AI's role in empowering English language teachers and learners in Korea*. The 36th KOSETA (Korean Secondary English Teachers Association) Academic Forum (2024, January 30-31), Busan, Korea.

Kozulin, A. (1986). Vygotsky in context. In L. *Vygotsky Thought and language (newly revised and edited by A. Kozulin)*, (pp. *xi-lvi*). The MIT Press.

Krashen, S. D. (1985). *The input hypothesis: Issues and implications*. Longman.

Krashen, S. D. (1995). *Principles and practice in second language acquisition*. Phoenix ELT. (Original work published 1982)

Krizhevsky, A., Sutskever, I., & Hinton, G. (2017). ImageNet classification with deep convolutional neural networks. *Communications of the ACM, 60*(6), 84-90. https://doi.org/10.1145/3065386

Kroll, J. A. (2020). Accountability in computer systems. In M. D. Dubber, F. Pasquale, & S. Das (Eds.), *The Oxford handbook of ethics of AI*. (pp.181-196). Oxford University Press. https://a.co/d/7jDMrif

Kukulska-Hulme, A., Lee, H., & Norris, L. (2017). Mobile learning revolution:

Implications for language pedagogy. In C. A. Chapelle & S. Sauro (Eds.), *The handbook of technology and second language teaching and learning* (pp. 217-233). Wiley Blackwell. https://a.co/d/7jDMrif

Kurzweil, R. (2005). *The singularity is near: When humans transcend biology.* Penguin Books.

Laird, J. E. (2019). Introduction. In H. A. Simon, *The sciences of the artificial, reissue of the third edition with a new introduction by John Laird* (pp. ix-xvi). The MIT Press. https://a.co/d/dWfuRQa

Lantolf, J. (2005). Sociocultural and second language learning research: An exegesis. In E. Hinkel (Ed.), *Handbook of research in second language teaching and learning* (pp. 335-353). Lawrence Erlbaum Associates.

Lantolf, J., & Beckett, T. G. (2009). Sociocultural theory and second language acquisition. *Language Teaching, 42*(4), 459-475.

Larson, G. A. (Writer), Souza, S. E. (Writer), & Stanley, P. (Director). (1982, November 19). Trust doesn't rust (Season 1, Episode 9) [TV series episode]. In G. A. Larson (Executive Producer), *Knight Rider*. Glen A. Larson Productions; Universal Television.

Lear, J. (1988). *Aristotle: The desire to understand.* Cambridge University Press. https://a.co/d/9filLeW

LeCun, Y., Bengio, Y., & Hinton, G. (2015). Deep learning. *Nature, 521*, 436-444. https://doi.org/10.1038/nature14539

Lee, H., & Lee, J. H. (2024). The effects of AI-guided individualized language learning: A meta-analysis. *Language Learning & Technology, 28*(2), 134–162. https://hdl.handle.net/10125/73575

Lee, P., Goldberg, C., & Kohane, I. (2023). *The AI revolution in medicine: GPT-4 and beyond.* Pearson. https://a.co/d/dgl3Cg2

Leone, S. (Director). (1966). *The good, the bad and the ugly* [Film]. MGM.

Levy, M., & Stockwell, G. (2006). *CALL dimensions: Options and issues in Computer-Assisted Language Learning.* Lawrence Erlbaum Associates.

Li, F. (2023). *The worlds I see: Curiosity, exploration, and discovery at the dawn of AI*. Flatiron Books: A Moment of Lift Book. https://a.co/d/cEXIRre

Li, F. (2024, April). *With spatial intelligence, AI will understand the real world* [Video]. TED Conferences. https://www.ted.com/talks/fei_fei_li_with_spatial_intelligence_ai_will_understand_the_real_world?subtitle=en

Liang, W., Yukekgonul, M., Mao, Y., Wu, E., & Zou, J. (2023). GPT detectors are biased against non-native English writers, *Patterns*, *4*, https://doi.org/10.1016/j.patter.2023.100779

Lightbown, P. M., & Spada, N. (2006). *How languages are learned* (3rd ed.). Oxford University Press.

Lighthill, J. (1973). *Artificial Intelligence: A general survey*. Science Research Council. https://www.aiai.ed.ac.uk/events/lighthill1973/lighthill.pdf

Lighthill Debate. (1973, July). *Controversy: The general purpose robot is a mirage*. [Documentary; online Video]. BBC. http://www.aiai.ed.ac.uk/events/lighthill1973

Liao, Q. V., & Vaughan, J. W. (2023). AI transparency in the age of LLMs: A human-centered research roadmap. *arXiv*. https://arxiv.org/abs/2306.01941

Long, M. H. (1983a). Linguistic and conversational adjustments to non-native speakers. *Studies in Second Language Acquisition*, *5*(2), 177-193.

Long, M. H. (1983b). Native speaker/non-native speaker conversation and the negotiation of comprehensible input. *Applied Linguistics*, *4*(2), 126-141.

Mahari, R., & Pataranutaporn, P. (2024, August 5). We need to prepare for 'addictive intelligence.' *MIT Technology Review*. https://www.technologyreview.com/2024/08/05/1095600/we-need-to-prepare-for-addictive-intelligence

McCarthy, J (2000, June 13). *Review of "Artificial Intelligence: A general survey."* http://jmc.stanford.edu/artificial-intelligence/reviews/lighthill.pdf

McCarthy, J., Minsky, M., Rochester, N., & Shannon, C. E. (1955). *A proposal for the Dartmouth summer research project on Artificial Intelligence*. http://raysolomonoff.com/dartmouth/boxa/dart564props.pdf

McClelland, J. L., & Rumelhart, D. E. (Eds.) (1986). *Parallel distributed processing: Explorations in the microstructure of cognition (Volume 2: Psychological and biological models).* The MIT Press.

McClelland, J. L., Rumelhart, D. E., & Hinton, G. E. (1986). The appeal of parallel distributed processing. In D. E. Rumelhart & J. L. McClelland (Eds.). *Parallel distributed processing: Explorations in the microstructure of cognition (Volume 1: Foundations)* (pp. 3-44). The MIT Press.

McCulloch, W. S., & Pitts, W. (1943). A logical calculus of the ideas immanent in nervous activity. *The Bulletin of Mathematical Biophysics, 5*, 115-133.

McKinsey & Company (2024, April 2). What is generative AI? *McKinsey & Company* https://www.mckinsey.com/featured-insights/mckinsey-explainers/what-is-generative-ai

Meta. (2024, April 18). *Introducing Meta Llma 3: The most capable openly available LLM to date.* https://ai.meta.com/blog/meta-llama-3

Minsky, M., & Papert, S. A. (2017). *Perceptrons* (reissue of the 1988 expanded edition with a new foreword by Léon Bottou: An Introduction to Computational Geometry). MIT Press. (Original work published 1969)

Mitchell, M. (2024). Debates on the nature of artificial general intelligence. *Science, 383*(6689), 5-14. https://www.science.org/doi/10.1126/science.ado7069

Mitchell, M., Palmarini, A. B., & Moskvichev, A. (2023). *Comparing Humans, GPT-4, and GPT-4V On Abstraction and Reasoning Tasks.* arXive. https://doi.org/10.48550/arXiv.2311.09247

MIT Technology Review. (2023, May 3). *Video: Geoffrey Hinton talks about the "existential threat" of AI* [Video]. https://www.technologyreview.com/2023/05/03/1072589/video-geoffrey-hinton-google-ai-risk-ethics

Mittelstadt, B. (2023). Interpretability and transparency in Artificial Intelligence. In C. Véliz (Ed.), *The Oxford handbook of digital ethics.* (pp.378-408). Oxford University Press. https://a.co/d/6i2W2X8

Moniz, J. R. A., Krishnan, S., Ozyildirim, M., Saraf, P., Ates, H. C., Zhang, Y., Yu, H., & Rajshree, N. (2024). ReALM: Reference resolution as language modeling. *arXiv:2403.202329*. https://doi.org/10.48550/arXiv.2403.20329

Morris, M. R., Sohl-dickstein, J., Fiedel, N., Warkentin, T., Dafoe, A., Faust, A., Farabet, C., & Legg, S. (2024). Levels of AGI for operationalizing progress on the path to AGI. *Proceedings of the 41st International Conference on Machine Learning (ICML) 2024*, Vienna, Austria. https://doi.org/10.48550/arXiv.2311.02462

Mun, S. K., & Koh, D. (2022). Special issue: Machine learning for computer-aided diagnosis in biomedical imaging, *Diagnostics*, *12*, 1331. https://doi.org/10.1016/j.patter.2023.100779

Mollman, S. (2022, December 10). ChatGPT gained 1 million users in under a week. Here's why the AI chatbot is primed to disrupt search as we know it. *Fortune*. https://fortune.com/2022/12/09/ai-chatbot-chatgpt-could-disrupt-google-search-engines-business/?utm_source=search&utm_medium=advanced_search&utm_campaign=search_link_clicks

Nelson III, C. A., Thomas, K. M., & Haan, M. D. (2006). Neural bases of cognitive development. In D. Kuhn & R. S. Siegler (Eds.), *Handbook of child psychology volume two: Cognition, perception, and language* (6th ed.) (pp. 3-57). John Wiley & Sons, Inc.

Novak, M. (2013, October 15). The computer doctor every '80s kid was promised. *GIZMODO*. https://gizmodo.com/the-computer-doctor-every-80s-kid-was-promised-1442633709

Novelli, C., Taddeo, M., & Floridi, L. (2023). Accountability in artificial intelligence: what it is and how it works, *AI & Society*, https://doi.org/10.1007/s00146-023-01635-y

O'Donnell, J. (2024, September 17). *MIT Technology Review*. https://www.technologyreview.com/2024/09/17/1104004/why-openais-new-model-is-such-a-big-deal

Omar, M., Ullanat, V., Loda, M., Marchionni, L., & Umeton, R. (2024, July 9). ChatGPT for digital pathology research. *Lancet Digit Health.* https://doi.org/10.1016/S2589-7500(24)00114-6

OpenAI. (2024a, May 13). *Introducing GPT-4o* [Video]. YouTube. https://www.youtube.com/watch?v=DQacCB9tDaw

OpenAI. (2024b, May 13). *Hello GPT-4o.* https://openai.com/index/hello-gpt-4o/

OpenAI. (2024c, May 14). *GPT-4.* https://openai.com/index/gpt-4-research

Ornes, S. (2024, February 13). How quickly do large language models learn unexpected skills? *Quantamazine.* https://www.quantamagazine.org/how-quickly-do-large-language-models-learn-unexpected-skills-20240213

Otto, S. E. K. (2017). From past to present: A hundred years of technology for L2 learning. In C. A. Chapelle & S. Sauro (Eds.), *The handbook of technology and second language teaching and learning* (pp. 10-25). Wiley Blackwell. https://a.co/d/elWEDq8

Overgoor, G., Chica, M., Rand, W., & Weishampel, A. (2019). Letting the computers take over: Using AI to solve marketing problems, *California Management Review, 61*(4), 156-185. https://doi.org/10.1177/0008125619859318

Ozdemir, S. (2023). *Quick Start Guide to Large Language Models: Strategies and Best Practices for Using ChatGPT and Other LLMs.* Addison-Wesley Professional. https://a.co/d/0dX4wWu6

Pack, A., & Maloney, J. (2023). Using generative artificial intelligence for language education research: Insights from using OpenAI's ChatGPT. *TESOL Quarterly, 57*(4), 1517-1582. https://doi.org/10.1002/tesq.3253

Pack, A., & Maloney, J. (2024). Using artificial intelligence in TESOL: Some ethical and pedagogical consideration. *TESOL Quarterly, 58*(2), 1007-1018. https://doi.org/ 10.1002/tesq.3320

Paletta, L., & Rome, E. (Eds.) (2022). *Attention in cognitive systems: Theories and systems from an interdisciplinary viewpoint* (4th International Workshop on Attention in Cognitive Systems, WAPCV 2007). Springer-

Verlag Berlin Heidelberg. https://a.co/d/04psM8Rma

Park, E. S. (2011). Learner-generated noticing of written L2 input: What do learners notice and why? *Language Learning, 61*(1), 146-186.

Park, P. S., Goldstein, S., O'Gara, A., Chen, M., & Hendrycks, D. (2024, May 10). AI deception: A survey of examples, risks, and potential solutions. *Pattern, 5*(5), 1-16. https://doi.org/10.1016/j.patter.2024.100988

Partridge, D. (1987). The scope and limitations of first generation expert systems. *Future Generation Computer Systems, 3*(1), 1-10. https://doi.org/10.1016/0167-739X(87)90038-0

Paul G. Allen School. (2024, January 21). *How we see and what we value: AI with a human perspective – Fei-Fei Li (Standford University)* [Video]. YouTube.
https://www.youtube.com/watch?v=gzOwpEupP5w

Patel, D. (2023, March 27). *Ilya Sutskever (OpenAI Chief Scientist) - Building AGI, Alignment, Spies, Microsoft, & Enlightenment* [Video]. YouTube. https://www.youtube.com/watch?v=Yf1o0TQzry8

Pedhazur, E. J. (1997). *Multiple regression in behavioral research: Explanation and prediction* (3rd ed.). Wadsworth.

Pennington, M. C. (1996a). The power of the computer in language education. In M. C. Pennington (Ed.) *The power of CALL* (pp.1-14). Athelstan Publications

Pennington, M. C. (Ed.). (1996b). *The power of CALL*. Athelstan Publications.

Pica, T. (2005). Second language acquisition research and applied linguistics. In E. Hinkel (Ed.), *Handbook of research in second language teaching and learning* (pp. 263-280). Lawrence Erlbaum Associates.

Piccinini, G. (2020). *Neurocognitive mechanisms: Explaining biological cognition*. OUP Oxford. https://a.co/d/07vfMAYw

Pinker, S. (2009). *How the mind works*. W. W. Norton & Company. (Original work published 1997). https://a.co/d/gpd3az2

PKETA & GETA. (2024). *AI-based English language education: Challenges and opportunities*. 2024 PKETA (Pan-Korea English Teachers Association) and GETA (Global English Teachers Association) Joint Conference (2024, June 15), Busan, Korea.

Prince, S. J. D., (2023). *Understanding Deep Learning*. The MIT Press. https://a.co/d/fuZ5HF8

Rizk, N. (2020). Artificial intelligence and inequality in the middle East: The political economy and inclusion. In M. D. Dubber, F. Pasquale, & S. Das (Eds.), *The Oxford handbook of ethics of AI*. (pp.625-649). Oxford University Press. https://a.co/d/7jDMrif

Roivainen, E. (2023, July/August). AI's IQ: ChatGPT aced a test but showed that intelligence cannot be measured by IQ alone. *Scientific American*, 7.

Rosenblatt, F. (1958). The perceptron: A probabilistic model for information storage and organization in the brain. *Psychological Review, 65*(6), 386-408.
https://doi.org/10.1037/h0042519

Ruder, S. (2018, October 1). A review of the neural history of natural language processing. *Quantexa*. https://aylien.com/blog/a-review-of-the-recent-history-of-natural-language-processing?ref=ruder.io

Rumelhart, D. E., Hinton, G. E., & Williams, R. J. (1986). Learning representations by back-propagating errors. *Nature, 323*, 533-536.

Rumelhart, D. E., & McClelland, J. L. (Eds.) (1986). *Parallel distributed processing: Explorations in the microstructure of cognition (Volume 1: Foundations)*. The MIT Press.

Russell, B. (1997). *Religion and science: With a new introduction by Michael Ruse*. Oxford University Press. (Original work published 1935)

Russell, B. (1972). *A history of western philosophy*. Simon & Schuster, Inc. (Original work published 1945).

Russell, S. (2019). *Human Compatible: Artificial Intelligence and the Problem of Control*. Penguin Books. https://a.co/d/fvFCY6p

Russell, S. J. & Norvig, P. (2010). *Artificial intelligence: A modern approach* (3rd ed.). Prentice Hall.

Russell, S. J. & Norvig, P. (2021). *Artificial intelligence: A modern approach* (4th ed.). Pearson. https://a.co/d/9ZGE1Bt

Sana. (2024a, May 15). Sana AI Summit 2024, Stockholm, Sweden. https://sanalabs.com/events/sana-ai-summit-2024

Sana. (2024b, May 20). *Geoffrey Hinton | On working with Ilya, choosing problems, and the power of intuition* [Video]. YouTube. https://www.youtube.com/watch?v=n4IQOBka8bc

Sapolsky, R. M. (2017). *Behave: The Biology of Humans at Our Best and Worst.* Penguin Books. https://a.co/d/6AAdNfu

Schmidt, R. W. (1990). The role of consciousness in second language learning. *Applied Linguistics, 11*(2), 17-46.

Schumacker, R. E., & Lomax, R. G. (2010). *A beginner's guide to structural equation modeling* (3rd ed.). Routledge.

Searle, J. R. (1980). Minds, brains, and programs. *Behavioral and Brain Sciences, 3*(3), 417-457. https://doi.org/10.1017/S0140525X00005756

Seung, S., & Yuste, R. (2012). Neural networks. In E. R. Kandel, J. H. Schwartz, T. M. Jessell, S. A. Siegelbaum, & A. J., Hudspeth (Eds.), *Principles of neural science* (5th ed.) (pp. 4214-4268). McGraw Hill/Medical. https://a.co/d/0308pAyO

Shadlen, M. N., & Kandel, E. R. (2021). Nerve cells, neural circuitry, and behavior. In E. R. Kandel, J. D. Koester, H. M. Sarah, S. A. Siegelbaum, & A. J. Hudspeth (Eds.), *Principles of neural science* (6th ed.) (pp. 56-72). McGraw Hill/Medical. https://a.co/d/bpW8VAn

Shah, P (2023). *AI and the future of education. Teaching in the age of artificial intelligence.* Jossey-Bass. https://a.co/d/bZZJMX9

Shakespeare, W. (1997). *Hamlet* in the Norton Shakespeare based on the Oxford edition: Tragedies (S. Greenblatt, W. Cohen, J. E. Howard & K. E. Maus, Eds.). W. W. Norton & Company, Inc. (Original work published 1603)

Sharwood Smith, M. (1993). Input enhancement in instructed SLA. *Studies in*

Second Language Acquisition, 15(2), 165-179.

Shin, D., & Lee, J. H. (2023). Can ChatGPT make reading comprehension testing items on par with human experts? *Language Learning & Technology, 27*(3), 27-40. https://hdl.handle.net/10125/73530

Simon, H. A. (2019). *The Sciences of the Artificial, reissue of the third edition with a new introduction by John Laird*. The MIT Press. https://a.co/d/dWfuRQa (Original work published 1969)

Singer, G. (2023, December 7). The history of the modern graphic processor. *TECHSPOT*. https://www.techspot.com/article/650-history-of-the-gpu

Smith, N. (1999). *Chomsky: Ideas and ideals*. Cambridge University Press.

Standford eCorner. (2024, May 2). *The possibilities of AI [Entire talk] – Sam Altman (Open AI)* [Video]. YouTube. https://www.youtube.com/watch?v=GLKoDkbS1Cg

Steven, M. S., & Luczaj, J. A. (2014). *Earth system history* (4th ed.). Freeman/Worth. https://a.co/d/08Hulv3F

Stevens, J. P. (2002). *Applied multivariate statistics for the social sciences* (4th ed.). Lawrence Erlbaum Associates, Inc.

Strang, G. (2016). *Introduction to linear algebra* (5th ed.). Wellesley-Cambridge Press.

Strategic computing initiative. (2023, March 16). In *Wikipedia*. https://en.wikipedia.org/wiki/Strategic_Computing_Initiative#cite_note-FOOTNOTERolandShiman20022-1

Sutskever, I. (2023, October). *The exciting, perilous journey toward AGI* [Video]. TED Conferences. https://www.ted.com/talks/ilya_sutskever_the_exciting_perilous_journey_toward_agi

Swain, M. (1985). Communicative competence: Some roles of comprehensible input and comprehensible output in its development. In S. Gass & C. Madden (Eds.), *Input in second language acquisition* (pp. 235-253). Newbury House.

Sykes, J. M. (2017). Technologies for teaching and learning intercultural competence and interlanguage pragmatics. In C. A. Chapelle & S. Sauro (Eds.), *The handbook of technology and second language teaching and learning* (pp. 118-133). Wiley Blackwell. https://a.co/d/elWEDq8

Takahashi, D. (2023, January 13). Got It AI creates truth checker for ChatGPT 'hallucinations'. *VentureBeat*. https://venturebeat.com/ai/got-it-ai-creates-truth-checker-or-chatgpt-hallucinations

The Alan Turing Institute. (2023, December 22). *The Turing Lectures: The future of generative AI* [Video]. YouTube. https://www.youtube.com/watch?v=2kSl0xkq2lM

The Francis Crick Institute (n.d.). *About Dr Francis Crick*. https://www.crick.ac.uk/about-us/our-history/about-dr-francis-crick

TIME. (1983, January 3). *Machine of the year: The computer moves in*. https://time.com/vault/year/1983

Tonelli, G. (2021). *Genesis: The story of how everything began*. Farrar, Straus and Giroux. https://a.co/d/9CINLER

Truscott, J., & Sharwood Smith, M. (2011). Input, intake, and consciousness. *Studies in Second Language Acquisition*, *33*(4), 497-528.

Turing, A. M. (1950). Computing machinery and intelligence. *Mind*, *59*(236), 433-460.

Tyldum, M. (Director). (2014). *The imitation game* [Film]. The Weinstein Company.

University of Oxford. (2024, February 29). *Prof. Geoffrey Hinton – "Will digital intelligence replace biological intelligence?" Romanes Lecture* [Video]. YouTube. https://www.youtube.com/watch?v=N1TEjTeQeg0

University of Toronto. (2023, June 23). *The Godfather in Conversation: Why Geoffrey Hinton is worried about the future of AI* [Video]. YouTube. https://www.youtube.com/watch?v=-9cW4Gcn5WY

UN News. (2024, May 30). *AI for Good Summit: Digital and technological divide is no longer acceptable*. https://news.un.org/en/story/2024/05/1150451

UPI. (1958, July 8). New Navy device learns by doing. *The New York Times.*

Vaswani, A., Shazeer, N., Parmar, N., Uszkoreit, J., Jones, L., Gomez, A. N., & Kaiser, Ł. (2017). Attention is all you need. *Proceedings of the 31st Conference on Neural Information Processing Systems, Long Beach, CA, USA.* https://doi.org/10.48550/arXiv.1706.03762

Vector Institute. (n.d.). *Geoffrey Hinton.* https://vectorinstitute.ai/team/geoffrey-hinton

Wang, Q., & Gayed, J. M. (2024). Effectiveness of large language models in automated evaluation of argumentative essays: finetuning vs. zero-shot prompting. *Computer Assisted Language Learning,* 1-29. https://doi.org/10.1080/09588221.2024.2371395

Warschauer, M. (1999). *Electronic literacies: Language, culture, and power in online education.* Lawrence Erlbaum Associates.

Warschauer, M., & Healey, D. (1998). Computers and language learning: An overview. *Language Teaching, 31*(2), 57-71.

Warschauer, M., & Kern, R. (Eds.) (2000). *Network-based language teaching: Concepts and practice.* Cambridge University Press.

Warschauer, M., & Xu, Y. (2024). Generative AI for language learning: Entering a new era. *Language Learning & Technology, 28*(2), 1-4. https://hdl.handle.net/10125/73569

Wei, J., Tay, Y., Bommasani, R., Raffel, C., Zoph, B., Borgeaud, S., Yogatama, D., Bosma, M., Zhou, D., Metzler, D., Chi, E. H., Hashimoto, T., Vinyals, O., Liang, P., Dean, J., & Fedus, W. (2022). Emergent abilities of Large Language Models. *OpenReview,* https://openreview.net/forum?id=yzkSU5zdwD

White, L. (2003). *Second Language Acquisition and Universal Grammar.* Cambridge University Press.

Williams, R. (2024, July 12). AI can make you more creative – but it has limits. *MIT Technology Review,* https://www.technologyreview.com/2024/07/12/1094892/ai-can-make-you-more-creative-but-it-has-limits

Wilson, E. O. (1999). *Consilience: The unity of knowledge.* Vintage.

Wolfram, S. (2023). *What is ChatGPT doing ⋯ and why does it work?* Wolfram Media, Inc. https://a.co/d/3j1nPwF

Woo, D. J., Susanto, H., Yeung, C. H., Guo, K., & Fung, A. K. Y. (2024). Exploring AI-generated text in student writing: How does AI help? *Language Learning & Technology, 28*(2), 183–209. https://hdl.handle.net/10125/73577

Zhao, H., Andriushchenko, M., Croce, F., & Flammarion, N. (2024). Is in-context learning sufficient for instruction following in LLMs? *arXive.* https://doi.org/10.48550/arXiv.2405.19874

Zizu. (2018, October 5). Dartmouth workshop: The birthplace of AI. *Medium.* https://medium.com/rla-academy/dartmouth-workshop-the-birthplace-of-ai-34c533afe992

Appendix

In physics, two distinct types of quantities are clearly differentiated.

> [Quantities] such as the velocity of an object, the force acting on it, ⋯, which have both magnitude and direction. Such quantities are called *vectors*; contrast them with such quantities as mass, time, or temperature, which have magnitude only and are called *scalars*. (Boas, 2006, p. 82, italic in original)

In mathematics, particularly in linear algebra, multiple numbers are represented and calculated simultaneously in horizontal and/or vertical alignments (cf. Strang, 2016). When numbers are arranged vertically, this configuration is referred to as a "**column vector**," or simply a vector (Strang, 2016, p. 2, bold in original). For those unfamiliar with physics and mathematics, it may be confusing that the same term, *vectors*, is used in two related yet distinct fields. It can also be challenging to understand how the concept of vectors is both practically and conceptually useful, although their meanings remain consistent across both disciplines.

As Boas (2006) explains, *vectors*, by definition, have two distinct pieces of information: 'magnitude' and 'direction.' When we say that something has a direction, it refers to its orientation within one, two, or three dimensions. If two things have different directions within the same dimension, they are considered distinct. In other words, vectors are

> a combination of algebra and geometry, which is important

> in many applications... Problems in various fields of science and mathematics involve the solution of sets of linear equations. This sounds like algebra, but it also has a useful geometric interpretation. (Boas, 2006, p. 82)

Similarly, Strang (2016) illustrates, ""You can't add apples and oranges." In a strange way, this is the reason for vectors" (p. 11, quotation marks in original). Graphically, vectors are represented as an arrow line. Strang (2016) further explains,

> A vector with two components [i.e., numbers] corresponds to a point in the *xy* plane. The components of the vector are the coordinates of the point: x = [the 1st number] and y = [the 2nd number]. The arrow ends at this point ([the 1st number, the 2nd number]). Now we allow vectors to have three components ([the 1st number, the 2nd number, the 3rd number]). The *xy* plane is replaced by the three-dimensional *xyz* space. (p. 11)

The following excerpt helps to further understand the complexities of processing text and how the transformer model manages it:

> [This] introduces transformers. These were initially targeted at natural language processing (NLP) problems, where the network input is a series of high-dimensional embeddings representing words or word fragments. Language datasets share some of the characteristics of image data. The number of input variables can be very large, and the statistics are similar at every position; it's not sensible to re-learn the meaning of the word 'dog' at every possible position in a body of text. However, language datasets have the complication that text sequences vary in length, and unlike images, there is no easy way to resize them. ⋯ To motivate

the transformer, consider the following passage:

> The restaurant refused to serve me a ham sandwich because it only cooks vegetarian food. In the end, they just gave me two slices of bread. Their ambiance was just as good as the food and service. [37 words]

The goal is to design a network to process this text into a representation suitable for downstream tasks. For example, it might be used to classify the review as positive or negative or to answer questions such as "Does the restaurant serve steak?"

> We can make three immediate observations. First, the encoded input [for the passage above] can be surprisingly large. In this case, each of the 37 words might be represented by an embedding vector of length 1024 [meaning, 1024 numbers are aligned], so the encoded input would be of length 37x1024 = 37888 even for this small passage. A more realistically sized body of text might have hundreds or even thousands of words, so fully connected neural networks are impractical.
>
> Second, one of the defining characteristics of NLP problems is that each input (one or more sentences) is of a different length; hence, it's not even obvious how to apply a fully connected network. ... Third, language is ambiguous; it is unclear from the syntax alone that the pronoun it refers to the restaurant and not to the ham sandwich. To understand the text, the word it should somehow be connected to the word restaurant. In the parlance of transformers, the former word should pay *attention* to the latter. This implies that there must be connections between the words and that the strength of these connections will

> depend on the words themselves. Moreover, these connections need to extend across large text spans. For example, the word their in the last sentence also refers to the restaurant. (Prince, 2023, pp. 377-378, quotation marks and italic in original)

According to Strang's (2016) explanation, adding a component (i.e., a single number) to a vector is equivalent to adding a dimension: two numbers define a 2D plane, and three numbers create a 3D space. Prince (2023) illustrates this with an example where 37 words are transformed into a vector of length 1024, situating them in a 1024-dimensional space. This level of dimensionality is practically impossible for humans to visualize and can only be understood conceptually; however, ChatGPT processes it faster than the blink of an eye. The challenge of managing more than three dimensions is not confined to laypeople, as shown in the following anecdotes from leading AI scholars:

> Our computer display devices (screens or paper) are two-dimensional, which means that it is easy to visualize two-dimensional data. And our eyes are experienced at understanding three-dimensional data that has been projected down to two dimensions. But many data sets have dozens or even millions of dimensions. In order to visualize them we can do dimensionality reduction, projecting the data down to a map in two dimensions (or sometimes to three dimensions, which can then be explored interactively).[17]

---

17 Geoffrey Hinton provides the helpful advice "To deal with a 14-dimensional space, visualize a 3D space and say 'fourteen' to yourself very loudly."
(Russell & Norvig, 2021, p. 708, footnote number and quotation marks in original)

Index

Kwang Hee Hong

Kwang Hee Hong holds a Ph.D. from Ohio State University in second language education. He is a professor in the Department of English Education at Yeungnam University, Korea. As a researcher and author, he specializes in Computer-Assisted Language Learning (CALL), L2 education, and quantitative research methods in applied linguistics, with publications in journals such as CALICO, ReCALL, English Language Teaching, and Multimedia-Assisted Language Learning. His research interests include L2 learners' motivation, CALL, and CALL teacher education. Recently, his focus has expanded to exploring the integration of AI into language education.